Baltimore & Ohio E-Unit Diesel Passenger Locomotives

Douglas B. Nuckles
with
Thomas W. Dixon, Jr.

B&O RR Hist. Soc. Coll.

New EA & EB No. 51 and 51X units at La Grange, Illinois plant in 1937.

1994
TLC Publishing, Inc.
Route 4 - Box 154
Lynchburg, Virginia 24503-9711

Dedication

This book is dedicated to the men whose responsibility it was to operate and maintain Baltimore & Ohio E-Series diesel passenger locomotives over the B&O Railroad system from 1937 to 1971.

Acknowledgements

Sincere thanks are due to a good friend, Tom Dixon, for the encouragement and inspiration for me to do this book. A great deal of sincere appreciation is herewith extended to all those who were helpful to me in obtaining information and photographs for this book, and for careful editing and suggestions: Thomas A. Biery, Ann Calhoun, Frank H. Dewey, Harry Eck, Herbert H. Harwood, Jr, John J. Holt, William F. Howes, Jr., Robert L. Hundman, Archie W. McElvany, Robert Malinoski, Louis A. Marre, Bruce A. Meyer, James Mischke, Diane D. Nuckles, and Nicolas C. Powell.

Library of Congress Catalog Number 93-61711
ISBN 1-883089-06-9

Typography and Layout by
Doug and Diane Nuckles

Printed in the United States by
Walsworth Publishing Co. Inc.
Marceline, Missouri 64658

Contents

Foreword

One may well ask, "Why a book on one class of diesel locomotives on one railroad?" This is a legitimate question in this era of proliferating books on the subject of railroading. It should be answered at the outset. There are several reasons why Baltimore & Ohio EMD E-series diesel locomotives should be deserving of treatment: First, the E-unit itself was the most common passenger train locomotive of the 1945-1971 era. Secondly, the B&O was a major user of E-units as one of the trunk-line railroads connecting the Northeast with the Midwest, scheduling important trains over a variety of heavily traveled routes. Finally, in 1935 B&O was a pioneer in the use of passenger trains with flexible consists hauled by diesel locomotives (along with the AT&SF) in the period when diesels were mounting their first serious challenge to steam power, and carried on with the model through its entire development and refinement through the E9 model in 1955. As such the B&O E units represent a microcosm of this locomotive's use and importance in the American railroad scene. One must not forget the conservative, tasteful blue/gray livery applied to these units, long a favorite of train watchers and modelers. They are among the most attractive of a class of locomotives that was given to expressive design, ranging from the gaudy to the mundane, on a variety of railroads,

Antipathy to lightweight equipment was, according to most sources, a prejudice of Daniel Willard. Actually, B&O entered the lightweight streamliner era quite early, in 1935, with *The Royal Blue* and *The Abe Lincoln.* Prominent in B&O's promotional literature throughout the late 1930s, and into the late 1940s, was the slogan "Diesel Powered All the Way!"

When TLC Publishing asked if I would consider putting together a book on Baltimore & Ohio E-Units, I was flattered. Even though I had been writing professional articles for many years, I had just finished my first railroad book. To be asked to do another before the first was on the shelves meant, to me, that I must have done something right.

Having grown up in eastern Chesapeake & Ohio territory, I hadn't seen many B&O E-units until very late in their lives, therefore not at their shiniest and newest. Even so, E units had always been among my favorites; therefore, it was an intriguing challenge to prepare this book.

From the 1950s to the 1970s E-units from several railroads were visible in Virginia, even B&O units on the C&O in later years just before Amtrak. However, my strongest impression of early B&O E-units is from visits to the B&O Railroad Museum in Baltimore, and a lengthy look at EA number 51, even though the paint scheme isn't totally accurate. Just as this book is being published E8 No. 92 is being moved to the museum as well. Eventually it will be returned to the wonderful blue/gray paint scheme and will become a new and important artifact reflecting the days when the E-units dominated railroad passenger train service on the B&O and in America.

Over a period of years, I painted many HO models of diesel locomotives. Among those I saw regularly in and around Richmond were several E8As including Atlantic Coast Line, Seaboard Air Line, Chesapeake & Ohio, Southern, and Richmond, Fredericksburg & Potomac. Several times I thought that I should do one in B&O, but never did. Perhaps this book may make up for my lack of previous attention to the road which used my favorite historic colors—blue and gray—along with serviceable black and gold striping.

We have attempted to research B&O E-units as thoroughly as possible, to bring the story of these locomotives to our readers in the most readable and useable form, and to secure the best available photographs to illustrate them on the Baltimore & Ohio.

Reference notes are given paranthetically after the data that they pertain to in the text. The notes are numbered sequentially and appear at the end of the book. If more than one reference applies all will be shown. A roster of each model appears in the photo section that pertains to that model rather than a consolidated roster for the entire fleet. A general renumbering of B&O locomotives occured in 1957, during which time the E-units were consolidated in sequential numbers in the 1400 series.

A section is devoted to the standard paint scheme most familiar on B&O E-units and its variations from the EA's through the E9s, but no attempt has been made to note the several later schemes and the many variations of them, although photos of most variations are shown. Basically, about the time of the C&O affiliation the E-units began to be painted solid blue with large yellow lettering, the same as C&O/B&O freight locomotives. A major variation of this is the "sunburst" scheme, which had several yellow "rays" extending from a centered B&O herald on the nose door. The final version was that which was ultimately adopted for both C&O and B&O E-units about 1967, with a solid blue body with broad a gray band covering about one-third of the side from the sill up.

Although there is much detail on the birth of the E-unit as a type, and its early use on the B&O, little definitive information has become available to us on the latter-day use of the newer E7, E8, and E9 models. This may be a result of the fact that by then the diesel locomotive is an "off the shelf" standard model, basically alike on all railroads that used it, and generally unremarkable in its performance on a particular line, unlike steam, which was tailored to a specific railroad and often a specific portion of that line.

Douglas B. Nuckles, DDS, MAT
Charleston, South Carolina
January, 1994

Introduction to B&O E-Units

In the period from World War II until the end of privately operated passenger trains in America, the EMD E-unit, more than any of its competitors, came to represent the streamlined passenger train, the ultra-modern embodiment of the century-old mode of travel most familiar to Americans. It ushered in the modern era of passenger train travel and it was venerable E6s, E7s, and younger E8s and E9s that hauled all the great and lesser trains on their final runs. B&O's ultimate ownership of 79 E-units (including the 7 units transferred to it from C&O in 1967), placed it high in the company of railroads operating these famous locomotives, in which Union Pacific and Pennsylvania Railroad led (155 and 134 units respectively). Because B&O was the first railroad to have the E-unit, the EA of 1937, and to buy some of the last of the model, the E9s of 1955, it encapsulates the entire history of this locomotive model from its earliest development on grueling grades on several of its most important runs, often substituting steam and later other diesel helpers for the stiffest climbs. These locomotives hauled some of the most highly respected and well-patronized trains in America from the late 1930s until Amtrak, including *The Capitol Limited, The National Limited, The Diplomat, The Ambassador, The Shenandoah, The Royal Blue,* and many more.

During the Great Depression of the 1930s, industrial design became an increasingly important element in American manufacturing as designers deftly added aesthetic features to all types of practical and commonly used items, from vacuum cleaners to locomotives. The newer industrial designers were influenced by the "modern" styles developed by the Bauhaus School of Design in Germany beginning in 1919, and the "Art Deco" style of decoration popularized at the 1925 *L'Exposition des Arts Decoratifs et Industriels Modernes* in Paris. In addition to new locomotives and trains, airplanes, particularly the then new DC-3, extended the airlines' routes to new horizons. For the mobile public, streamlined PCC trolley cars added improved styling and faster movement to work or pleasure travel over rails in the streets. Beginning with the Chicago, Burlington & Quincy's *Zephyr* in 1934, which captivated Americans with its "streamline" design and diesel power, and the Union Pacific's M-10000 train of similar design, the age of the streamlined train had begun.

The Baltimore & Ohio Railroad, along with most other railroads, maintained a continued interest in passenger train steam motive power well into the 1930's. The steam locomotive was still the workhorse, hauling daily passenger trains across the United States. Streamlined trains were an innovation. The railroads needed a diesel locomotive that could pull the load, regardless of whether it was a few coaches or a complete streamlined train, merely by adding more units, working together harmoniously as a single locomotive. The earliest streamliners had a fixed consist, permanently attached to the diesel locomotive, which was sized to handle the load of the integrated train only, not allowing the flexibility possible with standard trains.

The solution was a powerful diesel unit that could be coupled with other locomotives and could pull standard trains, just as steam locomotives did. The "box cab" design, if it could be called that, created by Richard Dilworth of Electro-Motive Corporation, was just a pair of diesel engines mounted in a box with traction motors driving the wheels. It was mechanically successful, but had drawbacks. Locomotive engineers objected to being up-front in the cab, in a low position. Engineers and firemen preferred to sit in elevated seats above the normal floor position, which provided better visibility and also better protection in case of a collision. Obviously, the boxy appearance did not blend with the new, lightweight passenger car equipment fast appearing on the rails. These early diesel locomotives were anything but streamlined.

Following incorporation on August 31, 1922 at Cleveland, Ohio, Electro-Motive Engineering Corporation continued its rail motor car business. In June 1930, General Motors Corporation purchased Electro-Motive, which went on to develop early diesel locomotives, the earliest being a 900 horsepower distillate-engined train. Continuing a progressive attitude, Electro-Motive Division (its new name) built a new locomotive shop at La Grange, Illinois, in 1935. After constructing two experimental diesel-powered demonstrator passenger locomotives in 1935, (Nos. 511 and 512) powered with Winton engines, EMD inaugurated the E-Series of diesel passenger locomotives in 1937 with the first EA model, No. 51.

Baltimore & Ohio's No. 51, model EA, was the first streamlined locomotive to emerge from EMD's La Grange, Illinois, plant. Early units were fairly standard with a long sloping nose and an engineer's cab high above the rails. The new streamlined units rode on new A1A-type trucks designed for them, with two powered axles and a center idler axle. As designs improved, new models appeared, and B&O used them all, constantly improving its fleet of streamlined passenger locomotives, placing them on every named passenger train on its rails. Santa Fe and B&O, using EMD's E-series, moved the streamlined passenger train from the integrated fixed-consist of the first streamliners into the modern passenger train that survives to the present.

Brief History of the Baltimore & Ohio Railroad

The first common carrier railroad in the United States was the Baltimore & Ohio Railroad. Located near the center of east coast shipping ports, B&O was the first railroad to provide both scheduled passenger and freight service. B&O was expected to build a railroad from Baltimore to some suitable location on the Ohio River to provide a means of developing traffic with the Midwest. (1-3)

The first serious talks about constructing a railroad in Baltimore were held in the summer of 1826. On February 27, 1827, the Maryland legislature approved a charter for the B&O, which was officially organized in April 1827. A year later the company adopted a route from Baltimore along the Potomac River. The first stone was laid July 4, 1828. (1,2)

By October 1829 the first track was laid from Pratt Streeet in Baltimore to Carrollton Viaduct. In December of that year both Patterson and Carrollton Viaducts were opened, and in April 1832 the railroad was completed to Point of Rocks, Maryland. Construction of the famous Thomas Viaduct, named for the B&O's first president, Phillip E. Thomas, and the Washington Branch started in July 1833, with completion of the Viaduct on July 4, 1835. (1,2)

A bridge across the Potomac River to Harpers Ferry, (West) Virginia, was completed in 1837. This important connection allowed the B&O to connect with the Winchester & Potomac Railroad. Track was completed to Cumberland, Maryland in November 1842, followed by completion of the Baltimore coal piers and the Locust Point Branch in July 1849. The Washington D.C. station was finished in the fall of 1852. In 1851 the Northwestern Virginia Railroad Company was chartered by the Virginia legislature, later becoming the Parkersburg Branch of the B&O. (1-3)

Building through Cumberland, Maryland, and Grafton, (West) Virginia, the railroad finally reached Wheeling, Virginia (not West Virginia until 1863) in January, 1853, after 25 years of construction, 379 miles from Baltimore. In November 1854 B&O opened a rail connection to Columbus, Ohio, and points west of there, via the acquired Central Ohio Railroad. In May 1857, B&O gained access to Cincinnati and St. Louis upon completion of the Northwestern Virginia Railroad, and a celebrated excursion train was first run (via two independent railroads with different gauges) from Baltimore to St. Louis and return in June 1857. As the road reached Chicago Junction, now Willard, Ohio, one of its subsidiaries continued to build on to Chicago, about 1874. (1-3)

B&O acquired other lines, by lease or joint operation, and also ventured to New York (actually Jersey City), in competition with the Pennsylvania Railroad. B&O constructed the first electrified mainline in the United States through the Howard Street Tunnel in downtown Baltimore.

In spite of being a large coal handler in the 1880's, B&O went into receivership in 1896. However, it emerged under its original charter in 1899. Then through stock acquisitions Pennsylvania gained control for almost ten years.

Louis A. Marre Coll.

Cumberland, Maryland was one of the first important points reached in the early construction of the B&O Railroad. The city grew as the railroad prospered. In 1947 E6A&B are in charge of the train, as an employee holds a stop sign.

In 1910 Daniel Willard was elected president. Very progressive in labor relations and steam development—later diesels and streamliners, he coordinated some important acquisitions, including the Baltimore & Ohio Chicago Terminal, formerly the Chicago Terminal Transfer Railroad, and the Coal & Coke Railway in West Virginia. As a result of the merger plan of the 1920s, B&O expanded even more, purchasing several lines between 1926 and 1943. (1,2)

For many years B&O was in direct competition with Pennsylvania and New York Central. Although B&O was first to buy diesels, it was slow to become fully dieselized. Many passengers preferred B&O trains over Pennsy's trains between Washington and New York (Jersey City), even though the B&O trains operated on a slower schedule. B&O encouraged travel from New York to the Midwest, including Chicago and St. Louis. Many travelers to the Midwest preferred to go via Washington, and even lay over for a day or two, finding the B&O's service and accommodations to be superior to other road's. (1,2)

By 1960 B&O was again in financial difficulty. Both Chesapeake & Ohio and New York Central acquired B&O stock, aiming for control of the faltering line. By 1962 the ICC and B&O stockholders approved of C&O control and within two years C&O owned 90 per cent of B&O stock. Later the ICC approved C&O control of the Western Maryland Railway. On June 15, 1973, Chessie System was created. Under Chessie System, Baltimore and Ohio, Chesapeake & Ohio, and Western Maryland were never corporately merged. Chessie System, Inc. was a holding company, whereas the *Chessie System* was a marketing trademark and not a corporate name.

B&O, as a one-third component, maintained an identity within Chessie System.

The last chapter in this story is the creation of CSX Transportation. Chessie System was combined with the SCL Industries (itself a consortium of Atlantic Coast Line, Seaboard Coast Line, Louisville and Nashville, and Clinchfield Railroads) in 1980 under a holding company called CSX. In 1987 these two, and all their subsidiaries, were merged into CSX Transportation. This was the real beginning of loss of identity for B&O, as all of the existing locomotives were repainted, albeit into several paint schemes. The present CSXT roster makes no differentiation between origins of locomotives, and does not attempt to identify their former railroad.

Many structures on the Baltimore & Ohio railroad are famous, but none more so than the Thomas Viaduct with its eight arches. Designed by Benjamin Latrobe in the 1820s, the structure was completed in the early 1830s. It was the first of many links necessary to connect Baltimore with Washington, D.C. Located at Relay, Maryland, the great viaduct was named for the B&O's first president, Phillip E. Thomas. The gently curved structure, constructed of granite blocks, with double track for the main line, crosses the Patapsco River nine miles south-southwest of B&O's downtown Mount Royal Station. Even after 160 years in service the Thomas Viaduct remains in service without ever having had major repairs or reinforcement. This famous location has been photographed over many years by the railroad for publicity photos, and by railfans for nostalgia and memoirs.

H. H. Harwood, Jr.

One of the Baltimore & Ohio 's noted streamliners, The *Capitol Limited*, is making its last eastbound run across the famous Thomas Viaduct on May 1, 1971. The two locomotives are ex-Chesapeake & Ohio E8s, with the lead unit No. 1461, ex-C&O 4011. Note that the first five cars match the locomotives in paint schemes, and there are two dome cars on this day. Amtrak had no place for the *Capitol* for over ten years after this Spring date in 1971.

F. R. Kern, Jay Potter Coll.

As the B&O expanded westward, it first connected with, then controlled, and finally absorbed the B&O Southwestern, which ran across Ohio and Indiana to St. Louis. Here E7A No. 1432 and E6B No. 2408 pause at Chillicothe, Ohio's impressive station/office building on July 4, 1957. Note that the exterior appearance of the B-unit has been much modified, with only one porthole left and E8-style stainless steel grills in place of the earlier style still demonstrated by the E7 ahead of it.

Louis A. Marre Coll.

St. Louis became the western terminus of the B&O, but the locomotive service facility was in East St. Louis, Illinois. In 1951 EA No. 55, rebuilt about 1945, crosses the diamond under the careful eye of the watchman, headed across the river to St. Louis.

Steam to Diesel Locomotive Transition

Twilight of Steam

The growth of the steam locomotive as a whole was possible only through the growth of its the component parts. Development of the basic elements was presented in considerable detail in Alfred Bruce's *The Steam Locomotive in America.* (4)

Some factors common to both types of locomotives, such as cost, fuel consumption, horsepower, tractive effort, and reliability were very important and caused some railroads to continue their research and development in steam beyond the introduction of the diesel-electric locomotive.

Baltimore & Ohio Railroad was an innovator and experimenter with steam locomotives from the earliest demonstration of the tiny *Tom Thumb* in 1830. Although the real spirit of the demonstration may have been lost in the locomotive's race with the gray mare from Relay to Baltimore, Maryland, the B&O directors were convinced of the practicality of steam locomotion; thus, the little experimental locomotive served its purpose well. (4)

Between 1837 and 1857 B&O leased its shops at Mt. Clare (Baltimore) to Ross Winans for the commercial production of steam locomotives. Winans built 0-4-0 type "grasshopper" engines, which had vertical boilers and cylinders connected to oscillating levers, with the rods connected to a horizontal jack shaft. Winans was considered to be a near genius in the design of early locomotives, although "experimenter" may be a better description. Some of his locomotive designs had names from the animal world, such as "crabs," "mud-diggers," and "camels." All of these had unique design features, which were considered successful in their time. He was devoted to producing locomotives with maximum tractive effort, and nearly all his designs were purchased by B&O. (4)

In 1903 American Locomotive Company (ALCO) began construction of the first compound articulated steam locomotive for B&O, an 0-6-6-0. Even though the details of building this type of locomotive varied over the years, the fundamental elements of construction remained almost unchanged.

Continuing its tradition of experimentation, B&O introduced the Emerson boiler in 1928, which had a firebox with a single top drum and side headers, from each of which two staggered rows of vertical tubes were connected to each of the two bottom side headers, quite unlike previous boiler designs. This was the largest installation of water-tube fireboxes to be made up to that time. (4,5)

In the mid-1930s Baltimore & Ohio was developing modernized streamlined passenger trains and had a keen interest in development of the emerging diesel-electric locomotive. But, at the same time, the B&O mechanical department was continuing its research in steam locomotive improvement.

Still feeling the effects of the Depression in 1934, B&O obtained a loan of $900,000 from the United States Public Works Administration, for the purchase of two high-speed lightweight streamlined trains and a diesel locomotive, No. 50, to be operated on daylight schedules. One of the two streamlined trains was to be powered by a steam locomotive and the other by the diesel. (5,6)

Bruce Fales, T.W. Dixon, Jr. Coll.

Baltimore & Ohio 4-4-4 No. 1, the first light-weight steam locomotive designed for high speed service at the same time that the early passenger diesel locomotive was being designed, as seen at Ivy City Yard, Washington, D.C., June 5, 1934.

The original B&O contribution to this project was a steam locomotive of advanced 4-4-4 type, designed especially for high speed service in connection with the new lightweight cars. It was completed at the Mt. Clare Shops in Baltimore that autumn and designated the *Lady Baltimore*, No. 1. Completed at Mt. Clare in January 1935, the *Lord Baltimore*, No. 2, a 4-6-4, was more powerful than the 4-4-4. Both locomotives were fitted with Emerson water-tube fireboxes combined with fire-tube boiler shells. Fireboxes included an unusually large proportion of the total evaporative-heating surface. (5)

The order for 16 lightweight cars went to American Car & Foundry in St Louis, Missouri. The two streamlined trains were different in that one was constructed of Cor-Ten steel and the other of aluminum on a lightweight steel framework.   Each train consisted of six cars with two spare cars for each train.

The two steam locomotives were not streamlined, although there was an attempt to place a shroud on the 4-4-4, but it was ordered removed before the installation was complete. Both locomotives rode on the largest drivers ever used on B&O locomotives, 84 inches in diameter. (5,6)

Comparison of Nos.	1	2
Railroad class	J1	V2
Wheel arrangement	4-4-4	4-6-4
Cylinders	17.5" x 28"	19"x28"
Driver diameter	84"	84"
Steam pressure	350 psi	350 psi
Weight on drivers	99,800 lbs.	156,000 lbs.
Total engine wt.	217,800 lbs.	294,000 lbs.
Tender wt.	170,000 lbs.	199,800 lbs.
Fuel, soft coal	14 tons	16 tons
Water,	8,000 gals.	10,000 gals.
Length, E&T	71' 4.5"	81' 6.5"
Tractive effort - engine	28,000 lbs.	34,000 lbs.
Tractive effort wBooster	35,000 lbs.	41,000 lbs
Date built	Fall 1934	Jan. 1935

Both locomotives made road tests hauling trains of about 250 tons, approximately equal to the weight of trains with six lightweight cars.   Operating on overall schedules of about 60 mph, including regular station stops and all operating checks and speed restrictions, both locomotives demonstrated the ability to meet the schedule requirements with top speeds slightly over 80 mph. This result was possible because of the high rate of acceleration in the medium and high-speed range. Hitherto, the class J-1 locomotive had served successfully on several divisions of the B&O system, making some exceptionally fast test runs on the Chicago division. At 95 mph, it developed 1,570 drawbar horsepower with a tractive force of 6,195 pounds. (5,6)

The fireboxes of both Nos. 1 and 2 were 159 inches long by 78 inches inches wide, fitted with five arch tubes. The length of the grate was reduced to 114 inches by a firewall extending up to the arch tubes. Both locomotives were equipped with stokers.

One particularly noticeable feature of these locomotives was the front-end door from which a multiplicity of clamp bolts was absent. A single lock and clamp, similar to those applied in British practice, secured the doors.

Both locomotives were built-up on cast-steel frames braced with welded cross-ties and a bolted cast-steel cradle at the rear end. The frames were fitted with cast-iron cylinders poured in the railroad's own foundry.   The steam pipes from the superheater headers to the cylinders, however, were of cast steel.

To conform with the cars, the rear of the tender on each locomotive was equipped with diaphragms which extended out to the roof and side lines.   Like the coaches, the tenders were fitted with Tight-Lock couplers and automatic connectors for steam and air as well as for the electric circuits. (5,6)

In order to make a pleasing, smooth front end, the pilot was arranged to protect and conceal the coupler, air piping, and hose when they were not in actual use. The front-end coupler pocket in the bumper casting was enlarged so that the coupler could be rotated horizontally about its pin until it was entirely enclosed within the pocket.

Both locomotives were also of lightweight construction, designed for both speed and economy in use with the lightweight trains. Before the two streamlined trains were placed in service, the B&O changed plans, assigned the Cor-Ten lightweight steel train to subsidiary Alton Railroad, and named it *The Abraham Lincoln*. The 4-4-4 locomotive, the *Lady Baltimore*, was assigned to that train.

The new *Royal Blue*, of aluminum construction was placed on the New York-to-Washington run to be hauled by the *Lord Baltimore* 4-6-4 locomotive. The single boxcab diesel locomotive, No. 50, was used alternately between the two trains for comparative purposes. (5,6)

All three of the locomotives proved successful from the standpoint of operating streamlined lightweight passenger trains on time. Even though the design appearance of the steam locomotives was

L.W. Rice, T.W. Dixon Coll.

Baltimore & Ohio 4-6-4 No. 2, the *Lord Baltimore*, with the new *Abraham Lincoln* on display on track 30 at Washington Union Station, May 27, 1935.

inconsistent with the new streamlined technology of the passenger car consists, the important point was established that a high horsepower diesel locomotive could easily substitute for steam locomotive passenger equipment of equivalent horsepower.

The Baltimore & Ohio Railroad built one 4-4-4-4 duplex type steam locomotive named the *George H. Emerson* in 1936-37, equipped with the Emerson water-tube firebox mentioned above. This locomotive, No. 5600, was Class N-1, with four cylinders, using single expansion, with a tractive effort of 65,000 pounds. The four single-expansion cylinders had an 18 inch bore and a 26-1/2 inch stroke. Each pair of cylinders drove two pairs of coupled wheels. Although comparison of the horsepower between a steam locomotive and a diesel was never considered exactly equivalent, No. 5600's cylinder horsepower was estimated to be around 3,900. This placed it 300 hp above the first road diesels, and it was claimed that this engine could outperform them in every way. (7,8)

feet 6 1/2 inches. Weight on drivers was 238,000 pounds. Total engine weight was 386,500 pounds and total engine and tender weight 736,500 pounds. (7,8)

The principal advantage of a locomotive of this type was its ability to provide 65,000 pounds tractive power with two pairs of cylinders and relatively light machinery, particularly those items entering into the counter-balance calculations. For instance, the weight of a main rod on locomotive No. 5600 was only 647 pounds compared with 1,512 pounds for a two-cylinder 4-8-2 type of the same tractive effort. There was also considerable reduction in the piston thrust. All of this tended to decrease the maintenance of the machinery and provide a smoother-riding locomotive. The comparative lightness of the locomotive in relation to its tractive power also gave it a favorable bridge rating. It could run anywhere on the B&O main lines. (7,8)

Tested on the Jersey City line for almost two years, the *George H. Emerson* was exhibited at the New York World's Fair in 1939. Later it worked between Willard, Ohio, and Washington, D.C., before being retired in 1943 and going to scrap in 1950. (7)

The earliest steam locomotives had a relatively short active service life due to their crude design and sometimes inadequate construction. The life span of steam locomotives became longer as art and skills increased, as may be seen in the Life Span of Steam Locomotives table on the following page.

B&O experimental 4-4-4-4 duplex No. 5600, the *George Emerson*, was placed on exhibition at the New York World's Fair in 1939—one of several designs which the B&O tried out in an effort to keep steam locomotives in use.

The Emerson 4-4-4-4 had four cylinders cast integrally with the engine frame. This casting was approximately 60 feet long, the first of this type ever produced with four cylinders. The cylinders were located one on each side immediately ahead of the driving wheels and one on each side behind the driving wheels. The front cylinders drove the first two pairs of drivers, their main rods connected to the second pair of drivers. The two rear cylinders drove the third and fourth pairs of drivers. The boiler of No. 5600, 80 inches in diameter, with a combined fire-tube and water-tube firebox, had a working pressure of 350 pounds. The driving wheels were 76 inches in diameter with 11 inch by 13 inch journals on the main axles and 10 inch by 13 inch on the other driving axles. Total engine and tender wheel base was 103

The duplex drive mechanism of B&O 4-4-4-4 type, the *George Emerson*, had two sets of drivers and cylinders, but was not articulated.

T. W. Dixon Coll.

LIFE SPAN OF STEAM LOCOMOTIVES (4)		
Period in which Locomotive was built	Life Cycle Falls between	Actual Service Life in Years
1830-1840	1830-1855	10-15
1840-1855	1840-1875	15-20
1855-1875	1855-1900	20-25
1875-1900	1875-1930	25-30
1900-1930	1900-1965	30-35
1930-1952	1930*	35-40
* To complete dieselization		

The Baltimore & Ohio Railroad, unique among major eastern railroads, experimented with innovative steam power to a greater extent than mentioned here, and to a greater extent than most railroads. Then, almost overnight, it seems, B&O decided to abandon further steam development and adopt diesel motive power for the future. This major decision must have been made by the highest level of management, most likely in 1936-1937, after careful deliberation and consultation with those directly involved with the day-to-day functions and operations of motive power.

Dawn of the Diesel

The diesel engine is an internal-combustion engine that uses the heat of highly compressed air to ignite a spray of fuel introduced after the start of the compression stroke. A diesel-type engine demonstrated by Briton Ackroyd-Smith, in the 1880's, was improved by Richard Hornsby & Co. of Grantham, England. (9)

However, Dr. Rudolph Diesel (1858-1913), a German engineer and inventor, is usually given credit as the inventor of the modern diesel engine. In 1898, he used a high-compression ratio to obtain a large increase in thermal efficiency of the engine, by injecting fuel with a blast of compressed air at 1,000 psi. (9)

McKeen gasoline powered motor cars were built as early as 1905, with about 150 of them produced. Not a threat to the steam locomotive, they were merely an early concept prior to the creation and design of the diesel-electric locomotive. They had a small power plant and a passenger compartment in a single car.

In 1936 there were over 900 motor cars using gasoline or oil as their primary fuel source. The primary reason for the decline in the use of gasoline as fuel in railroad motor cars was the very real fire hazard of gasoline. By 1948 there were only 472 motor cars still using gasoline as fuel. (4)

The diesel-electric locomotive is literally built around the diesel engine. The first *significant, separate, diesel-electric* road-type locomotives were produced in 1935 for use on both the Baltimore & Ohio and the Atchison, Topeka and Santa Fe railroads.

At the end of 1949, there were about 29,000 steam locomotives remaining on Class I railroads in the United States, only about 8,000 of them constructed in 1926 and after. Thus, there were about 21,000

active steam locomotives that were over 25 years old. Maintenance cost on these old locomotives was excessive in most cases. The following table shows railroads in the United States which reported more than 1,000 active steam locomotives in service in 1948:

U.S. RAILROADS WITH 1,000 OR MORE STEAM LOCOMOTIVES IN SERVICE IN 1948 (4)		
Railroad	No. of Steam Locomotives in Service Early 1948	No. of Route Miles of Track
Pennsylvania	4,467	9,736
New York Central	3,473	10,534
Baltimore & Ohio	2,030	6,192
Atchison, Topeka & Santa Fe	1,730	13,081
Southern Pacific	1,554	8,195
Southern	1,509	7,705
Illinois Central	1.324	6,581
Union Pacific	1,323	9,756
Milwaukee	1,213	10,359
Chesapeake & Ohio	1,208	5,076
Chicago & Northwestern	1,042	8,058
Chicago, Burlington & Quincy	1.030	8,867

The steam engine did not give in to the diesel without a fight. In the twilight days of steam many different locomotive types and experimental engines made their appearance. To name but a few, there were the famous 100-series streamlined Hudsons on the Milwaukee, the Niagaras on the New York Central, the Union Pacific Big Boys, C&O's 2-6-6-6, N&W's A-Class, and several Pennsylvania Railroad designs.

The transition from steam to diesel started during the greatest economic depression ever in the United States. But even during those hard times railroads were actively engaged in research looking for the best locomotive designs, regardless of the type of power used for locomotion. The chief competitor of the steam locomotive on U.S. railroads was obviously the diesel-electric.

This transition from steam power to diesel-electric power was not instantaneous, occurring over a span of years, not so much by design as by necessity. Although the gradual change from steam to diesel affected the lives of everyone associated with railroads, hurting some, by and large, this transition ultimately proved to be a boon to the railroad industry. It was therefore instrumental in improving the lives of many more people than it might have harmed.

As this transition continued into the late 1950's, one scene that continued to be a ritual on the B&O's Cumberland Division was the changing of steam motive power. Frank Shaffer described vividly the action of helpers at M&K Junction, West Virginia in a *Trains* magazine article. (6) Perhaps his closing sentence said it best — "The black-and-white of steam with its high costs is gone, along with the pageant of an era. Diesel blue has changed red ink to black." (10)

Richard Dilworth & Diesel Development

No book about the development of the diesel locomotive in the United States would be complete without a tribute to Richard Dilworth, such as in Franklin Reck's book *The Dilworth Story*. (11)

Born in Seattle, Washington Territory, in 1885, Richard McLean Dilworth was self-educated, largely through practical experience in a variety of jobs as varied as vagabond circus worker, printer, ship's cook, telephone lineman, and machinist, as well as a term in the Navy as an electrician on the Battleship *Kearsarge*. He was hired by General Electric in 1910 and began work on development of the gas-electric car for railroad application. In 1913 he worked on an experimental diesel engine GE was developing and proved successful in solving design problems associated with the early French and Swiss diesels. From 1914 to 1923 he was in the Phillipines, installing diesels at Fort Drum, and in 1923 returned to GE's gas-electric rail car operation.

Later, he became a liaison between General Electric and Electro-Motive, functioning as a consultant on electrical design problems. On January 1, 1926, Electro-Motive hired Dilworth as chief engineer. His career now was focused and remained so for the next 25 years. (12)

Following more work with the rail cars and distillate fuels, he eventually found himself working with the diesel locomotive, which was to be the answer for more speed, cost reduction, and greater efficiency for the railroads.

In 1930 General Motors acquired the Winton Company on June 30, and Electro-Motive on December 31. In conjunction with the Winton Company in 1932, General Motors Research developed a compact diesel engine, known as the 201. Although it was developed for use in Navy submarines, the 201 was a great advance in diesel design and construction. Two of these engines were placed in the Burlington Lines' *Zephyr*, in time for display at the Century of Progress Exposition at Chicago.

With the *Zephyr's* success, Dilworth and his two draftsmen were retained by Electro-Motive in an office in the Winton Engine Company in Cleveland, Ohio. He worked with railroads designing new "power cars." With a certain amount of ingenuity he steered the development of new diesel locomotives the way he wanted it — in the direction of uniformity. He was now devoted to the diesel and is quoted as saying, "I'm going to put this animal where it belongs if it takes all my life." (11)

The new, fast streamliners had their troubles but Dilworth and his men kept them rolling, proving the ability of the diesel locomotive to meet passenger schedules on a regular basis. However, although they made money, these trains had inflexible fixed-consists. Any car breakdown removed the entire train from service—an unacceptable consequence that had to change.

The obvious answer to this problem was to build separate, single-unit diesel locomotives to be coupled to the front end of standardized equipment. By this time power was no longer a problem. The time had come for the diesel locomotive to challenge steam power on the main line, on its own rails.

In 1934 diesel locomotives were still in a developmental stage. Because of the Depression, many railroads were in receivership and

EMC Boxcab locomotives Nos. 511 and 512 were demonstrated on a few railroads. Here they are seen trailed by an early dynamometer car with a heavy freight on the *Chicago, Burlington & Quincy* in Aurora, Illinois, on September 9, 1935.

thus had little money to risk on such new ventures. Electro-Motive was only a skeleton of its former strength. No one in the country was as qualified as Dilworth to proceed to the next step. He still had faith that someday a diesel locomotive would pull *The Twentieth Century Limited*.

In 1934 many railroads were trying hard to meet high-speed passenger schedules behind steam locomotives. But a steam locomotive heavy enough to pull a long train more than 70 miles per hour did one of two things. Either the drive wheels pounded the

Also, "Not until you talked about the speed at which the locomotive was to pull the train did you concern yourself with the horsepower. To arrive at this, you translated the weight of the locomotive into tractive effort, a figure expressed in pounds. You multiplied this by the desired speed in miles per hour, divided by 308, and you had the horsepower required in the desired diesel engine." (11)

No one said it better than Dilworth, "All railroading is based on one thing — that 1 horsepower equals 33,000 foot-pounds per minute. And you juggle that

Baltimore & Ohio EMC boxcab diesel No. 50 is waiting to depart Philadelphia, Pennsylvania with the westbound *Royal Blue* in August 1935.

W. R. Osborne, H. H. Harwood, Jr. Coll.

rails unmercifully, even leaving the track for a fraction of an inch, or the front of the locomotive began to sway back and forth. Trying to correct one fault resulted in accentuating the other. The conclusion was that the connecting rods and high drivers of the steam locomotive had to be eliminated. It was already known that there was a maximum size and speed beyond which a steam locomotive could not go. Many believed that Richard Dilworth was the man to change the way things would be. (11,12)

Dilworth decided to build a pair of experimental diesel locomotives that would outperform three of the best 4-6-4 type steam locomotives available. General Motors finally appropriated a half million dollars for him to build his two diesel locomotives. Although it appeared to be dubious at the time, this was one of GM's wisest investments.

Dilworth's theory was that, "Any locomotive could be reduced to a formula that required only arithmetic for its solution." Franklin Reck, in his biography of Dilworth, said, "From the railroad, you learned the weight of the train you would have to pull and the steepest grade you would have to pull it up. To these data you then applied certain simple formulas for train resistance and grade resistance, and you came out with the required weight of the locomotive." (11)

and toss it around and set it to music and play it on a flute. And you make it come out a locomotive." (11)

Concluding that the 3,600 horsepower necessary to better the performance of the 4-6-4 type steam locomotives, wasn't available from the 201A diesel engines, Dilworth decided to put diesel engines in boxcars! As he considered the boxcar to be a thing of simplistic beauty and a marvel of design, he put a pair of 900 horsepower Winton 201A V-12 engines into one. Since existing boxcars would not hold four diesel engines, he decided to put two engines into two coupled boxcars to get his 3,600 horsepower. He noted that, if uncoupled, each powered boxcar had 1,800 horsepower and separate controls, when and if, necessary. He was very proud of the fact that he "got a locomotive into a simple four-axle car." He accomplished all this while Electro-Motive was a stripped down subsidiary attached to the Winton Company. (11,12)

Electro-Motive's sales manager went to B&O's chief of motive power, hoping to convince him of the merits of the new diesel and elicit sales. At no cost to B&O, the new diesels were pitted against steam locomotives. For years railroads had been the real designers of steam locomotives. Dilworth wanted no more of that. He wanted a diesel locomotive suitable for all railroads without any single road preference. Both Santa Fe and Baltimore & Ohio placed orders after some disagreements. B&O box-cab No. 50 was constructed at Erie as were the ATSF units. At first, new diesel locomotives had considerable difficulty. Dilworth said "The 511 and 512 proved that a diesel locomotive couldn't be built and it wouldn't run—but when it did run, it would pull a train." (11)

B&O's chief of motive power had stated that it took a 5,000 horsepower steam locomotive to move a loaded freight train over Sand Patch Hill, a steep grade fifteen miles long. Dilworth was not satisfied until his new demonstrators (Nos. 511 and 512), with 3,600 horsepower, on its first run to Chicago, made the run with ease. Overwhelmed, Col. George Emerson, B&O's General Superintendent of Motive Power and Equipment, said of Dillworth's demonstrators, ". . . she's the pullingest animal on rails!" (11,12)

The net result of these tests was that Baltimore & Ohio's newest locomotive was put to work pulling the crack New York-Washington train, *The Royal Blue*, while Santa Fe's two units were placed on *The Super Chief* between Los Angeles and Chicago.

The new passenger locomotives entered service mid-to-late 1935. While they were being refined, Electro-Motive was building a new multi-million dollar plant at La Grange, Illinois. This plant became the largest diesel locomotive plant in history.

As new diesel locomotives were being refined for production at La Grange, steam engineers had their input, which resulted in the cab being moved up and back for safety purposes. This eliminated the boxcar look, but resulted in repositioning of the generator and diesel engine toward the middle of the frame. The portholes were the result of new truss construction in the sidewalls. Thus, mechanical improvements were related to new styling trends. (11,12)

With emergence of the Streamliners, as the latest diesel locomotives were known, the era of color arrived on U. S. railroads. Replacing the dark, drab steam locomotives, the new,

sleek design diesels were adorned in brilliant gold, red, yellow, and blue.

Dilworth referred to the newly painted passenger diesels as "circus wagons" and continued in his quest for functionality. He pointed out, "These streamliners were bought neither for their economy nor for their reliability. Nobody knew at the time whether they would save money, or stand up. They were bought for one purpose only, and that was speed." (11)

The new diesel locomotives proved to be more economical to operate than steam, and that they were available many more hours per year meant that they were even cheaper in original cost. As the railroads realized the savings, the diesel locomotive was prepared for a career in hauling freight.

Of considerable interest to steam and diesel enthusiasts alike, Dilworth described the losing battle of the steam locomotive:

"The only way to make a steam locomotive more powerful is to increase the number of square feet of heating surface in the boiler. Since tunnels and railway platforms and the width between rails all limit the height and width of an engine, the only way to increase the heating surface is to make the boiler longer. But if it gets too long, the fire gets cold before it reaches the far end of the boiler. Thus there is a practical limit to how large a steam locomotive can be." (11)

After the diesel passenger locomotives had proven themselves for more than a decade, Richard Dilworth began the task of building diesel powered freight locomotives. (11,12)

B&O No. 50 had lights and screens added, along with new lettering on its sloping nose, to accentuate its position with *The Abraham Lincoln*. Seen here at Chicago on June 18, 1937.   Louis A. Marre Coll.

Passenger Diesel Development in the 1930s

In the early days of diesel passenger locomotive development, the B&O subsidiary Alton Railroad's northbound *Abraham Lincoln* is powered by EA No. 50 and the boxcab booster, as it passes through Granite City, Illinois.   Walter Peters, R.R. Wallin Coll.

In September 1935 *Railway Age* reported on the "longest run ever made by a heavy, diesel-powered train of standard all-steel equipment," then recently completed, over the B&O by the twin unit diesel-electric locomotive (EMC 511-512) built by Electro-Motive Corporation for test service on American railroads. The record run was made from Jersey City, New Jersey to St. Louis, Missouri, 1,106 miles. Following a two-hour stop, the locomotive left St. Louis with a regular Alton Railroad train to Chicago for an additional run of 284 miles. (16)

On the run to St. Louis the locomotive hauled 10 standard steel cars, an average of 757 tons, and it pulled 12 cars of 808 tons from St. Louis to Chicago—impressive numbers for that time. The locomotive, weighing 250 tons, was described then as "the most powerful of its type yet placed in road service in this country." It consisted of two 1,800 horsepower units of identical construction.

Since the flexibility to modify consists and to add or subtract motive power as conditions required was a necessity, EMD developed a high-horsepower passenger diesel that could be coupled to any existing or standard train to haul it just like a steam locomotive. Thus was born the "boxcab" units that ATSF and B&O purchased, and which led directly to the creation of EMD's "streamlined" series of E-units starting with B&O and Santa Fe EAs of 1937. (27)

The external design of the Dilworth-designed boxcar bodies of Electro-Motive's Nos. 511 and 512 was considerably less attractive than that of the passenger cars which they hauled, which were increasingly of the streamlined type.

The first diesel passenger locomotive on the B&O, boxcab No. 50, an 1,800 horsepower single unit, accumulated over 560,000 miles, handling 545 pounds per horsepower starting in August 1935, first on the B&O, and later on the Chicago & Alton Railroad (at that time a subsidiary of the B&O).

It was also reported that this first road locomotive experienced some traction-motor armature-bearing failures and some trouble with connecting-rod bearings shelling out. The six 2-unit road locomotives (EA & EBs) had but one traction-motor armature-bearing failure, and two traction-motor axle-cap bearings heated in two years' operation. None of these caused any delay in service, according to a report from the B&O appearing in a 1939 *Railway Age* article. (14)

The B&O reported some problems with internal parts of diesel engines, such as rods, bearings, and pistons, but little or no delay occurred when it was necessary to cut out one of the locomotives. Minor problems also occurred with the traction motors, even though they were removed for routine repairs every 200,000 miles. The original connecting-rod bearings were being replaced with bronze bearings, which were expected to provide much longer service without failure. Wheels with heat-treated molybdenum gave an average life of 250,000 miles with two turnings. Considerable trouble was experienced at first with cylinder-head cracking, but this problem was reduced by the use of vent pipes, and regular removal of scale which prevented proper dissipation of heat from the cylinder heads, liners, and radiators.

Even though diesel orders began to surpass those of steam in the 1940s, the replacement of steam locomotives came about quite slowly. That rail fans and photographers disliked diesels during the closing days of steam was already apparent among members of the railroad press. Articles indicating locomotive production had a thread of apology for including diesels together with steam locomotives. Where complete trains were ordered, the diesel orders appeared only with the train order and were not noted along with locomotive orders. The Depression was slipping away, but it would take a while before the preoccupation with hard times would diminish.

The initial cost of the diesel locomotive was considerably higher than that of its steam counterpart, but when that cost was averaged over the number of miles operated through the years, the diesels overcame steam's original advantage. Maintenance costs appeared to be quite low on diesels, with the railroad press reporting 437,000 miles of operation for B&O E6 No. 56 with only three days out for repairs. The cost of water and water treatment for steam locomotives was quite significant when one compared operating costs of steam versus diesel locomotives. Fuel costs of the era were far lower than what exist today. Diesel fuel averaged only four cents per gallon in 1939; factored for inflation, it would cost much more in today's terms, but was still cheaper and easier to transport and store than coal. (14)

The following table illustrates the gain in popularity of diesel locomotives between 1929 and 1940.

Domestic Orders for Locomotives 1929-1940			
Year*	Steam	Diesel	Electric	Total
---	---	---	---	---
1929	1055	80	95	1230
1930	382	18	21	421
1931	62	21	91	174
1932	5	7	0	12
1933	17	25	0	42
1934	72	37	76	185
1935	30	60	7	97
1936	435	77	24	536
1937	173	145	36	354
1938	36	160	29	225
1939	95	246	32	373
1940	219	462	13	694

* In certain instances domestic orders placed in December are not reported until the following year. Statistics for years 1929-1939 have been revised to eliminate this overlap.

From the table one can see the general effect of the Depression on the railroad's purchase of new motive power, as shown by totals for the years 1931-1939. Note also the increasing trend to order diesel-electric locomotives beginning in 1937.

In order to put the early E-units into proper perspective, one must first look at the economic situation in 1937 to 1939. When these locomotives were first introduced, the Depression had started almost ten years before, and many were wondering if it would ever end. Statistics showed less reason for concern as locomotive orders and car loadings were showing a general, though somewhat gradual, increase. (13)

Locomotive orders in 1938 included 36 new steam locomotives, 29 electrics, and 163 diesels. The diesel category did not include "gas electric" motor cars. In 1939, orders were placed for 95 steam locomotives, 32 electrics and 248 diesel-electrics. The figures for 1940 were much higher than those of 1939 as the requirements of war production for our European allies began to be felt. Twenty new streamlined luxury passenger trains were introduced in 1939, bringing the total to 82 such trains. Thirteen of these were for use in the eastern half of the United States and seven for use in the western half. The traffic increased by 15 percent in freight car loadings from 1937 to 1938, and 6 percent for passengers. (13)

The figures for locomotive production in 1938 and 1939 show that the railroads had already begun a heavy swing to the diesel. This early swing was primarily due to the advantages of diesel locomotives in switching service. By January 1, 1940, 749 diesels were in service on 122 railroads with 33 percent of those less than one year old. Of those 749 units, only 44 were in the 2,000-horsepower or larger class.

The Baltimore & Ohio had a 600 horsepower diesel locomotive switcher which by 1939 had worked 18,650 hours in service since December, 1936, without general overhaul or major parts replacement.

Baltimore & Ohio was not happy with boxcar-like diesel locomotives which could not have been more out of character with their new streamlined passenger trains, and within two years, on June 18, 1937, placed a slanted nose on No. 50.

Electro-Motive's first worthwhile streamlined diesel was the EA, using a carbody design with sheet-metal skin and riding on six-wheel trucks (A1A type with center axle an idler). The letter "E" in the model designation originally stood for "eighteen," because the new model had 1,800 horsepower. When the designation stuck, the locomotives in the passenger "streamliner" series became known as the E-Series even though horsepower increased to 2,400. (40)

The basic carbody was rectangular with slightly curved roof and a curved nose slanting downward from the high cab at a 30-degree angle. The rear of the unit was flat and perpendicular to the sides. The cab windows were fitted into the curved cab design, much like an automobile windshield of the era. Each side had several flat windows, most of which had curved corners. The air horn was set conspiciously on the roof above the cab. Exhaust stacks were not visible from the ground close to the lcoomotive because they were quite short.

Although they were not streamlined in the same way as the Art Deco designs being developed by Otto Kuhler and Raymond Loewy, they were quite aestetic compared to the boxy designs of the early diesels.

Because of these good performance records and the railroad's desire to get into the "Streamliner" market, B&O ordered six EA and six EB units in 1937. (6) They were Class DP-2 and DP-2X. The cabless B-units were noted with an "X" following the Class numbers. On May 19, 1937 Baltimore & Ohio received its fist EA/EB set, Nos. 51 and 51X, from Electro-Motive. It was the first of two similar sets to be placed in service on *The Capitol Limited* between Washington, and Chicago, Illinois, shortly after June

1, 1937. The locomotive was inspected by several officers of B&O and EMD on May 19, and made its inaugural run the next day on a test run from Chicago to Washington. (17)

Sanat Fe Railway's first EA's went into service the previous day. As improvements and new developments occurred, the EA was followed by the Santa Fe E1A's and E1B's and the Union Pacific E2's. Several railroads purchased the E3 model, followed by the E4's, and a lone Chicago, Burlington & Quincy E5. The E6 model was the first *production* model.

The E7 was the model sold in the greatest quantity. Although the E8 is distinctively different in external appearance from the E7, most of the improvements were internal. The E9 model was identical to the E8 model outside, with a horsepower increase internally.

Originally intended to be semi-permanently coupled and treated as a single locomotive, the EAs and EBs were used on runs measuring 226 miles from Washington to New York, and 887 miles from Washington to St. Louis per day. These engines were serviced regularly, particularly at Washington, D.C., where an 8-hour layover occurred. Diesel engines were reconditioned on a schedule of assigned service of 50,000 miles. These six locomotives accumulated two million miles, with loads up to 894 pounds per horsepower, hauling 14 heavyweight passenger cars, using a steam locomotive helper for a short distance over Sand Patch Grade in the Allegheny Mountains, with an availability of 93.2 per cent, very good for such a railroad operation.

In January 1938, *Railway Age* reported that a pair of EAs, in service only several days, had taken the eastbound train at Washington, Indiana, which was running more than an hour late, and arrived in Parkersburg, West Virginia ahead of its scheduled time. (18)

The remaining EAs and EBs were delivered in early 1938 and assigned to the *Royal Blue* and the *Columbian*, (19)

On the occasion of placing modernized Pullman cars in service on *The Capitol Limited*, at a celebration in Washington, D.C., on November 23, 1938, the legendary actress, Tallulah Bankhead, "smashed" the traditional bottle of champagne against the nose of the Baltimore & Ohio's new EA as it led the new consist out of Union Station. *Railway Age* gave this event a lengthy account. (20)

On February 25, 1940, B&O EA No. 56 completed its 365th consecutive daily run between Chicago and Washington for a full year "without a miss." The locomotive had run a total of 280,000 miles with only routine maintenance. The performance was claimed to be a new all-time record for a 12-month period. The 772 mile Chicago-to-Washington run was scheduled for an average speed of more than 56 miles per hour, which included ten regular stops, over some of the heaviest mountain grades in the eastern United States. No. 56 arrived in the morning and departed the same afternoon, so that the longest period in which it stood idle was six and one-half hours—a marvelous feat for any locomotive. (21)

In September 1940 the B&O placed seven new E6A/E6B diesel locomotives into service (the A-B set was considered a single locomotive; there were seven A-units and seven B-units), hauling no less than five named trains, including *The Capitol Limited* and *The Shenandoah* between Washington and Chicago, *The National Limited* between Washington and St. Louis, *The Royal Blue* and *The Columbian* between Washington and New York, and *The Abraham Lincoln* of the Alton between Chicago and St. Louis. (22,23)

As rail traffic continued to increase and improve, B&O inaugurated diesel-powered passenger train service to Detroit in the fall of 1941. (24)

The Electro-Motive Division model E6 has been referred to as its first production diesel locomotive. Although the number of E6s produced (113 units) make the title a bit questionable, the E6 did have the distinction of being one of the first all-EMD products. The company's earlier policy was to use engines and various component parts produced by others, thus being primarily a carbody and locomotive assembler. World War II halted further production of the E6, and when passenger locomotive production resumed following the war, the EMD E7 with its bulldog nose, was the new design made available. (25)

Baltimore & Ohio Boxcab No. 50

Model No.: AA
Serial No.: 532
Date Built: August 1935
Engine type: Winton 201A (2)
Horsepower: 1800
Maximum speed: 98 mph
Min. continuous speed: 20 mcs
Gear ratio: 55:22

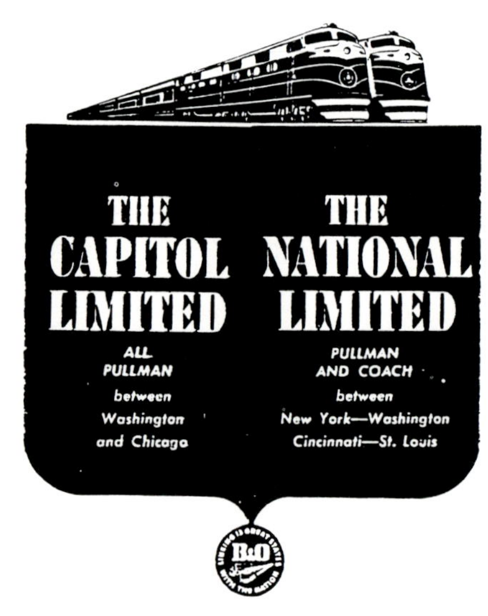

The B&O's Diesel Passenger Train Fleet in 1940

A presentation of the B&O's fleet of diesel-powered passenger trains appeared in the November 16, 1940 issue of *Railway Age*: (29)

The B&O operates a fleet of six modernized, streamlined, Diesel-electric-powered trains on four runs, the *Royal Blue*, the *Columbian*, the *Capitol Limited* and the *National Limited*. The present *Royal Blue*, rebuilt in the railway's Mt. Clare shops, replaced the new streamlined train of the same name that was found too small for the Jersey City-Washington run and which is now the *Abraham Lincoln* of the Alton. Operated with standard equipment, the *Columbian* was the first completely air-conditioned train, effective May 24, 1931. The *Capitol Limited* has long been an outstanding all-Pullman train. However, after deluxe coaches and a buffet-lounge for coach passengers had been installed on the *National Limited* in June of this year and proved successful, the *Capitol Limited* was similarly equipped on August 4, 1940, with immediate results in increased passenger revenues. In fact, it has frequently been necessary since to run a special coach section of the *Capitol* to take care of the business. This service has been particularly popular with Government employees going to and from Washington on pleasure travel or visits home. The descriptions of these trains follow:

<table>
<tr><td colspan="2">Capitol Limited (2 trains)</td></tr>
<tr><td>Weight of train:</td><td>2,900,820 lb.</td></tr>
<tr><td>Consist:</td><td>13 cars & twin power units;
1 postal, buffet-coach-lounge; 2 coaches; 3 bed-sect. cars;
2 drawing room cars;
2 section sleepers;
1 diner;
1 observation.</td></tr>
<tr><td>Placed in service:</td><td>May 13, 1923 (Standard)
Nov. 23, 1938 (Streamlined)</td></tr>
<tr><td>Operated between:</td><td>New York-Chicago</td></tr>
<tr><td colspan="2">Daily mileage per train: 996.2</td></tr>
<tr><td colspan="2">Overall scheduled speed: 48.6 M.P.H.</td></tr>
</table>

<table>
<tr><td colspan="2">National Limited (2 trains)</td></tr>
<tr><td>Weight of train:</td><td>2,491,000 lb.</td></tr>
<tr><td>Consist:</td><td>11 cars & twin power units
1 postal;
1 buffet-coach-lounge;
2 coaches;
2 drawing-room sleepers;
1 bedroom-section sleeper;
1 diner;
1 observation-lounge.</td></tr>
<tr><td>Placed in service:</td><td>April 26, 1935 (Standard)
June 28, 1940 Streamlined</td></tr>
<tr><td>Operated between:</td><td>New York-St. Louis</td></tr>
<tr><td colspan="2">Daily mileage per train: 1,110</td></tr>
<tr><td colspan="2">Overall scheduled speed: 44.1 m.p.h.</td></tr>
</table>

<table>
<tr><td colspan="2">Royal Blue (1 train);
Columbian (1 train)</td></tr>
<tr><td>Weight of train:</td><td>Royal Blue —1,937,600 lb.
Columbian — 1,908,260 lb.</td></tr>
<tr><td>Consist:</td><td>8 cars & twin power units;
1 baggage coach;
3 reclining chair coaches;
1 diner;
1 coach-tavern;
1 drawing-room parlor;
1 cafe-lounge-observation.</td></tr>
<tr><td>Placed in service:</td><td>Royal Blue—June 24, 1935
Columbian—June 16, 1929 (Standard)
Sept. 26, 1937 (Streamlined)</td></tr>
<tr><td>Operated between:</td><td>New York-Washington</td></tr>
<tr><td colspan="2">Daily mileage per train: 447</td></tr>
</table>

Both *The Royal Blue* and *The Columbian* made a round trip daily on alternate Washington runs and had the same consist, although *The Royal Blue* was a slightly heavier train.

The *Columbian* was actually the coach section of *The Capitol Limited*, containing an 8-section, 4-double-bedroom sleeping car between Pittsburgh, Pennsylvania, and Chicago. When eastbound, the *Columbian* left Chicago's Grand Central Station at 3:50 PM, 25 minutes before the departure of *The Capitol Limited*. The *Columbian* and *The Capitol Limited* were combined in Washington, D.C., and the combined train traveled to Jersey City, New Jersey with a 1:45 PM arrival. Westbound, the combined *Capitol-Columbian* passed over the famous Thomas Viaduct at Relay, Maryland, en route to Washington, DC. The westbound trains were split in Washington. *The Capitol* left at 4:30 and *The Columbian* leaving at 4:40 PM, due to arrive in Chicago at 7:10 and 7:20 AM.

Diesel Technology & Aesthetics

The Technological Argument

The technological argument for diesels was given very cogently by G. F. Gurley, Vice President of AT&SF in an article in Railway Age *in 1940. (15).*

"The principal characteristics of the Diesel-electric locomotive which have appealed to railroad managers in the operation of these high speed trains, are less static weight per wheel, particularly driving wheels, a reduction in unsprung weight, the complete elimination of dynamic augment, or the hammer blow incidental to the unbalanced forces of the reciprocating steam locomotive, the shorter wheel base for driving wheels, greater availability and lower fuel costs. The diesel has a thermal efficiency of about 27 per cent as compared with about 8 or 9 per cent for a gasoline engine.

Another advantage is that a Diesel-electric locomotive assists materially in narrowing the spread between the average speed and the maximum speed. This is possible because among other things less time is required for refueling and water, and as compared with a coal-burning steam locomotive there is the complete elimination of fire and ash-pan cleaning. Deceleration is faster with the diesels because it is possible to employ a higher braking ratio. It is common practice to utilize a comparatively low braking ratio on the drivers of steam locomotives. The tires of a steam locomotive are shrunk on and held in place by the force of contraction and it is poor judgment to attempt heavy braking action because of the dangerous possibility of a high degree of temperature on the tires of drivers. The diesel by lowered center of gravity may negotiate curves at a higher rate of speed than a steam locomotive.

The principal objection to the Diesel is increased capital investment — the cost per horsepower being about 2 1/2 or 3 times that of a steam locomotive. The greater availability of the Diesel locomotive, or in other words, the ability to produce more locomotive miles per year, reduces or in some instances may eliminate the investment handicap if the investment be considered a 'cost per locomotive mile per year' rather than merely the cost per locomotive.'

The Aesthetic Argument (by T. W. Dixon, Jr.)

The aestetic argument for the diesel, though it could not be quantified in thermal efficiency and cost-savings, was equally important in that the new sleek streamlined locomotives were a radical break with the cumbersome, smoke-belching, grimy steam locomotives that had come to symbolize an earlier day in the American experience. Streamlined diesels came at the same time that streamlined passenger cars arrived on the scene, and indeed the first streamlined cars and diesels were permanently coupled in sets such as the pioneering Union Pacific M-10000 and Burlington Route's *Zephyr.* Cars then began to be designed in full standard size but to "streamlined" appearance with smooth rooflines, large rounded-corner windows flush with the sides, and was made of new materials such as aluminum and stainless steel. These cars, painted in bright colors, made a striking appearance that was incongurous with a black steam locomotive, sprouting valves and pipes all-about at the lead. The automobile-like diesels, set in boxes with internal workings hidden could be styled outwardly to fit the sleek streamline image. The two were a perfect match for the railroads to use in changing the image of passenger travel. The B&O was unable to buy new lightweight streamlined cars because of its large debt, but it took many of its best standrad (or heavyweight) cars and put new sides and roofs on them, oplus skirting and new windows, and they gave the appearance of the streamliners, especailly since the new interiors were in keeping with the modern image as well. The B&O was particularly interested in having diesels haul these refurbished and redesigned trains to attract attention to them.

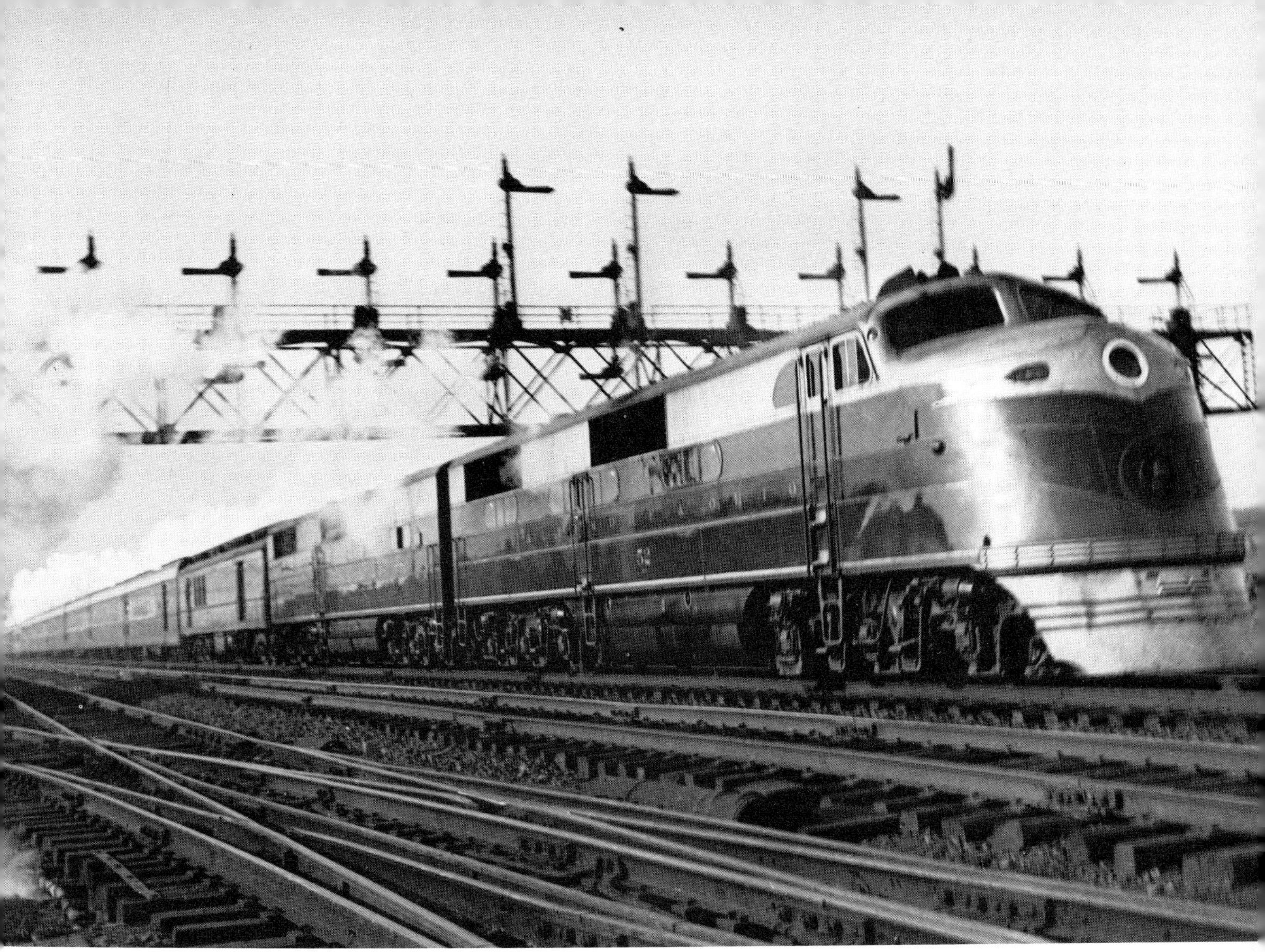

R. Malinoski

(Above) At speed near Jersey City, New Jersey, on a cold December 8, 1939, B&O EA/EB Nos. 52 /52X power train 26, *The Columbian*, one of the earliest B&O streamliners, with only the RPO car not matching.

(Below) B&O train No. 1, *The National Limited,* with E7AB No. 51 ahead of 4-6-2 No. 5316 and 9 cars backing past QN Tower at Washington, D.C. on July 20, 1947; the EAs had been in service almost exactly 10 years at that time.

E.L. Thompson, B&O RR Historical Society Coll.

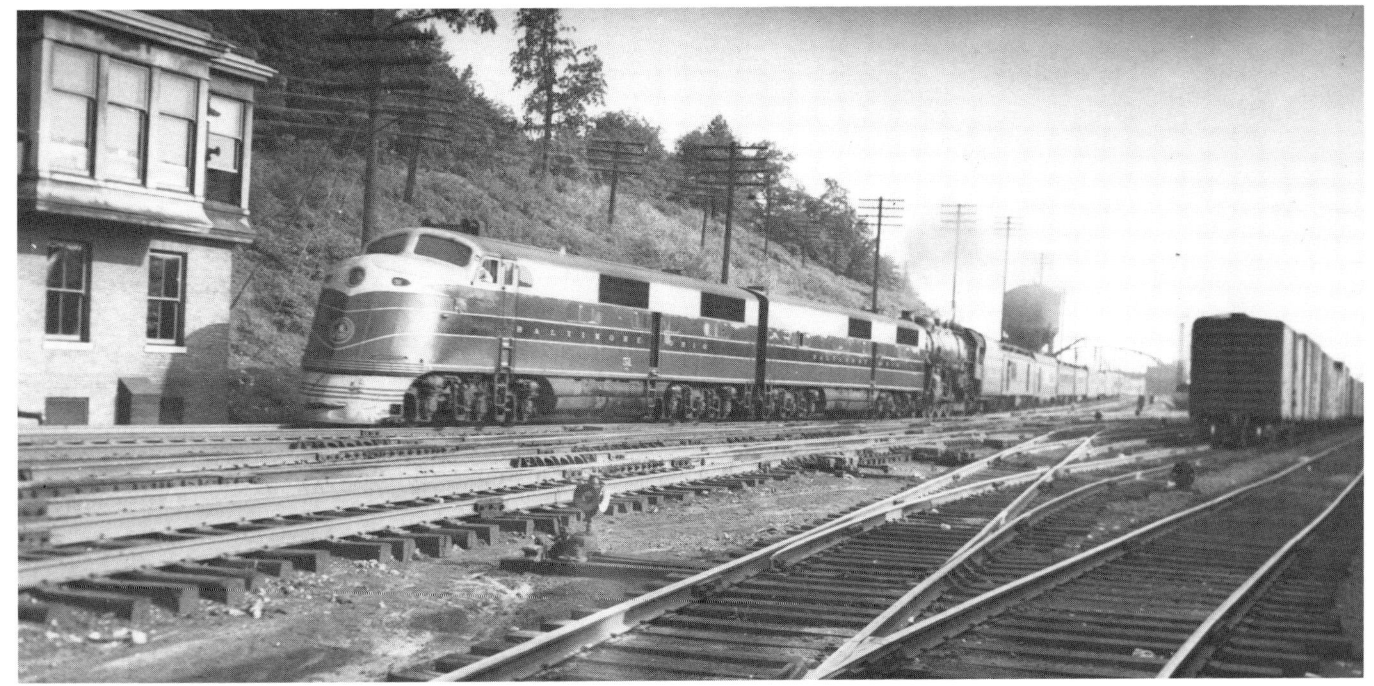

Northbound on the Alton Railroad, at the time a subsidiary of B&O, EA No. 50 has help from Boxcab No. 50 and 4-6-2 No. 5287 with *The Abraham Lincoln* near Springfield, Illinois. Date is unknown. Unusual is the fact that this photo shows the whole evolution of motive power on one train: steam-to-boxcab, diesel-to-streamliner!

B&O EA/EB No. 52 speeds *The Royal Blue,* one of four early streamliners on the B&O, beneath a semaphore signal bridge at Halethorpe, Maryland, under the careful eye of a tower operator.

Early B&O E-Units: Slant-Nose EAs & E6s

E6s, the Earliest Production Units

The E6A model was a natural advancement from the EA model; externally, they are very similar.

EMD's first serious efforts to establish themselves in the passenger locomotive market resulted in the EA, E1, and E2, followed closely by the E3 through E6.

The EA, E1, and E2 all shared the same carbody with minor differences, with the EA going to B&O, E1s to ATSF and the E2s to Union Pacific, Southern Pacific, and Chicago & Northwestern for the "City" trains. These locomotives, EA through E2, were built for just one year between May 1937 and June 1938. Then came the common carbody E3, E4, E5, and E6. E4s went to Seaboard Air Line, and E5s went to Chicago, Burlington & Quincy system. E6's went to a number of different customers. The first of these four classes to be shipped were the E4s to the SAL in October of 1938—production ending with Louisville & Nashville E6s in 1942. E3 production ranged from March 1939 to November 1939, E4s from October 1938 to November 1939, E5s from February 1940 to June 1941 and the EMD E6s from April 1940 to September 1942.

The E6 model was the first to be produced in large quantity, with 92 E6As and 26 E6Bs built between late 1939 and 1942. The production quantity of the E6, along with the mass production techniques of EMD, helped the E6 to become the first true production road diesel locomotive by Electro-Motive. A total of 118 E6s were sold to 14 different railroads before World War II cancelled the production of passenger locomotive motive power.

Most of the E6s were put into service with brand new streamliner trains. However, on the B&O, L&N, and Milwaukee Road, the E6s displaced existing steam locomotives or prevented the purchase of new steam locomotives.

When B&O ordered 14 of the new E6 model, it again considered sets of 2 units, an A and a B, a single 4,000hp locomotive. The B's carried the same number as the A's with an "X" suffix, thus the 57-59, 57X-59X were received in late 1940 and 60-63, 60X-63X in mid-1941. Of course war production limitations suspended production of domestic passenger diesels at that time. The E6 A&B's were classed DP-3 and DP-3X respectively by B&O, and remained active into the 1960s.

R. P. Wallis, H. H. Harwood, Jr. Coll.

(Left) Baltimore & Ohio EA No. 54 receives attention by crew and maintenance personnel at Ivy City Engine Terminal at Washington, D.C. in 1939. (Below) Maintenance workers are servicing B&O E6A&B No. 52 in Washington, D.C. This locomotive was fitted with a headlight visor which lasted for several years.

L. W. Rice, Louis Marre Coll.

Diesel Locomotive Supervisors

About 1941 (B&O Motive Power Dept. Bulletin dated 12/11/41), when early E-units were being delivered, EMD suggested B&O create the position of Diesel Electric Supervisor. A few other roads, such as the Santa Fe, are known to have had Diesel Electric Supervisors. These men, also known as "Diesel Riders," were responsible for all of the E-units in each passenger train locomotive consist, and they were also found on freight train locomotive consists.

According to one source, Diesel Riders did not exist in the B&O's Western Region before 1945. A retired Diesel Rider from the Western Region believes that the concept of using young machinists and electricians began with his group in 1946. Diesel Riders may have been in existence in the Eastern Region before 1946.

Of the three regions of the B&O, (Eastern, Central, and Western), the Western Region included five Divisions, and extended from Parkersburg, West Virginia, to East St. Louis, Illinois; from Louisville, Kentucky to Cincinnati, Ohio; from Cincinnati to Toledo (Detroit for passenger service); Cincinnati to Newark, Ohio, to Wheeling, West Virginia; Cincinnati to Indianapolis, Indiana to Decatur, Illinois.

Passenger service was dieselized from Parkersburg, to St. Louis. The Toledo Division passenger trains were operated by steam until the mid-1950s.

In the 1940s locomotive shops on the railroad were located at Cone (East St. Louis); Washington, Indiana; Stockyards (Cincinnati); Ivorydale; Chillicothe, Ohio; Parkersburg, West Virginia; Newark, Ohio; and Indianapolis, Indiana.

The performance of B&O diesel locomotives was exemplary. This is not to say that it was perfect, because evidence of locomotive parts failing included traction motors, steam generators, flat spots on wheels, fluid leaks, and low oil pressure, but none of that was due to lack of attention by Diesel Electric Supervisors. Creation of these positions, along with the fine performance of these dedicated men, probably was the decisive factor in the greater than 90 percent "On Time Rating" of B&O passenger trains in the 1940s.

Diesel Riders, assigned coverage on "line of road" freight and passenger locomotives, carried a set of hand tools to make any minor road adjustments possible, including mechanical (steam generator/boilers, air brakes) or electrical which could be repaired temporarily or permanently. They were responsible for continuing inspections on "line of road" and making reports on ICC Forms.

The Diesel Electric Supervisors were to report any condition on their locomotive(s) which could possibly develop into a future breakdown, and if serious enough, to send a wire to the Motive Power Department Office. These conditions also included flat spots on wheels, ground protective relay operation, low oil pressure, fluid leaks, and anything that might affect the safe operation of the locomotive.

An important further responsibility of the Diesel Rider was to ensure that engineers and firemen were educated in the operation of the locomotive and what to look for in anticipation of future or present problems.

The Diesel Electric Supervisors, (the Diesel Riders) played a very important and significant role in the successful maintenance and operation of B&O's diesel locomotives in the early 1940s to the 1950s, when the role was apparently dropped. These men, often working under arduous conditions, more than a few suffering loss of life in the performance of duty, contributed unheralded performances to keep B&O trains operating at their peak of performance.

Former Diesel Electric Supervisor in the Western Region, John J. Holt, offered the preceeding information. Mr. Holt was kind enough to provide a personal memoir, as well as several letters and bulletins which were published during his tenure as a "Diesel Rider." — By the 1960s virtually all motive power officials from Superintendent W. F. Dodd on down, had been Diesel Riders and had received this excellent field training, thus very well equipping them for their higher supervisory roles.

L.W. Rice, T.W. Dixon, Jr. Coll.

(Right) This pair of E7A's are about to be serviced in Ivy City at Washington, D.C. There are seven men—probably including the fireman, engineer, diesel rider, two mechanics by the first unit and two more about to enter the cab of the second unit—in this photo dated March 14, 1946, Efficient and regular service of passenger diesel locomotives enabled B&O to maintain a high level of on-time performance.

Baltimore & Ohio E7s, E8s, and E9s

Appearance and Operation of E7s, E8s, and E9s

Electro-Motive's 2,000 horsepower E7s were built between 1945 and 1949. A total of 407 E7As and 75 E7Bs were constructed. They were nearly identical to the E3, E4, E5 and E6 units which preceeded them except for the sorter less-slanted nose and a model 567A engine in place of the earlier 567 model.

Between 1949 and 1953, EMD built 454 of the 2,250 horsepower E8A's and 35 E8B's. They were distinctively different in external appearance from their predecessors. Although the noses of these two models were essentially identical, any view of the sides reveals the three large rectangular air intakes behind the "chicken wire" screen on the E7 and the two double and one single square window on each side, and the vertical louvers behind the cab door. The E8 and E9 had full-length stainless steel grillwork along the top of the carbody sides where the E7 "Chcken wire" was, and four round portholes on each side, when new. The numberboards were placed flush, whereas E7 numberboards protruded from the nose.

The lesser known E9 model, the last of the E-series which followed, was simply an improvement of the E8, having 2,400 horsepower per unit. The 93 E9As and 39 E9Bs were constructed between 1954 and 1964. Externally, the E9 was identical to the E8 model.

The operation of E8 locomotives with helper loco-

motives (presumably, this also applied to E9s) was clearly described in the 1951 *EMD E8 Enginemen's Operating Manual.* (35)

The speed of passenger trains in mountainous country is generally limited to 30 to 45 MPH, depending on track curvature and grade. In order to maintain a maximum speed of long heavy passenger trains, consistent with safety and passenger comfort, a helper locomotive is generally used over long continuous mountain grade.

Where practicable, it is generally advisable to climb a grade with wide open throttle in order that the time on the grade be kept as short as possible.

After the helper locomotive has been coupled on, the air brake equipment is set for double heading as in past practice. The Rotair valve on the second locomotive should be left in "PASS" to give engineman the use of independent brake valve. It is not necessary to cut out the electro-pneumatic brake. Both a standing and running brake test should be made from lead locomotive.

After starting, it is generally good practice to get the diesel locomotive into parallel as soon as practicable. The throttle may then be reduced to maintain desired speed.

If the grade is such that locomotive speed gets below minimum continuous speed, the throttle must be reduced to put more of a load on the helper locomotive.

The *Manual* explains further that when one is operating a Diesel locomotive as a helper unit in mountainous country, the procedures are basically the same as that for a steam locomotive helper.

A diesel locomotive that is used in helper service is generally geared for much lower top speed than that of a passenger diesel. Care must be exercised so that train speed does not exceed that of the locomotive geared for the lowest speed.

In the early days of the passenger diesel locomotive on the B&O, until the road was fully dieselized, diesel locomotive operations were contained east of Washington, Indiana. Diesels on westbound trains were taken off and placed on the next eastbound train. Eastbound trains out of St. Louis had the steam locomotives turned and returned west as soon as practical. At the time the B&O did not have an adequate number of diesels for all passenger trains. If the diesel locomotives were used through to St. Louis they would have to lay over one night and thus lose almost a full day of usefulness.

New B&O E8As Nos. 96 and 96A are at the Washington Terminal inspection pit on October 26, 1950.

Comparison of E7, E8, and E9s

The most obvious difference between the E7 and E8 models was in the position and orientation of the engines and main generators. In E7s, both prime movers faced to the rear of the locomotive carbody. The main generator on the end of each prime mover faced forward, toward the cab in the E7A units. In the E8s, the front prime mover was reversed so that the generator end faced forward. The governor ends of the two prime movers faced each other at the center of the locomotive. The location of both prime movers farther forward in the carbody opened up a space for the steam generator at the rear, separated from the engine room by a bulkhead. This allowed individual air filtering and temperature control in the carbody. The relocation of the prime movers was made possible by adoption of an accessory rack, which grouped the oil cooler, coolant expansion tank, oil filter tank, strainer housing, load regulator, and air compressor neatly and compactly around the front of each prime mover, near the center of the locomotive.

Grouped at the rear of each prime mover, on top of the main generator, was the main generator blower, auxiliary generator and traction motor blower, all powered from a common drive. In the E7 model individual supply accessories were mounted around the perimeter of the engine room, and engine driven accessories, such as air compressors and traction motor blowers were located forward and aft of the prime movers, anywhere power takeoff shafts and belt drives could reach them.

The battery compartment under the cab nose E7 was moved to the steam generator compartment in the E8s. Separate fuel and water tanks in the E7 were unified in an integral fuel/water tank in the E8, where the water compartment surrounds the fuel compartment, shielding it from rupturing if an accident should occur.

Another major revision involved the carbody air system. The E7 radiator air supply entered three inlets on each side of the carbody vented to eight 26" belt-driven fans mounted vertically in four pairs above, fore and aft of each prime mover. Air drawn through the fans passed upward through the radiator cooling cores and out the roof vents as regulated by sets of roof mounted shutters.

Two shop related weaknesses of this air system were 1) that considerable attention was required to maintain the belts properly, and 2) that false ceiling-access panels to the bottom of the cores had to be removed by shop personnel to gain headroom while working on the prime mover. Frequent failure to replace the panels vented fan output to the engine room rather than through the radiator cores, with resultant cooling loss.

On the E8 carbody, cooling air entered the carbody through eight side inlets located behind the stainless steel inlet grill. Four of these inlets were divided diagonally by carbody bracing; radiator shutters were located behind the grills. After passing through the shutters, air circulated upward through the radiator cores, drawn by the six 36" electric cooling fans mounted horizontally in the roof. The two outermost fans were hidden by the two winterization hatches whose function is explained later. The AC supply for the cooling fans was supplied by a companion alternator mounted directly to the main frame of the main traction generator. The cooling fans were controlled by automatic control switches, acting sequentially to bring more fans into service as the temperature rose.

E8 air intake for engine and equipment blowers was different. Located in the winterization hatch over each prime mover was a fourth 36" fan, similar to the three cooling fans, but which blew air downward through a filter compartment built into the roof hatch into the carbody. Oil wetted wire mesh cleaned the air just before it entered the engine room. This fan could draw air supply from either of two sources, from a duct through which air enters the carbody behind the stainless steel trim grill during summer, or in winter by a switch in the position of flaps inside the winterization hatch, it could draw warm air from the exhaust stream of the #1 radiator cooling fan.

Unfortunately, like many other devices, this air system could also be completely circumvented by the same negligence, failure to replace the "false ceiling"

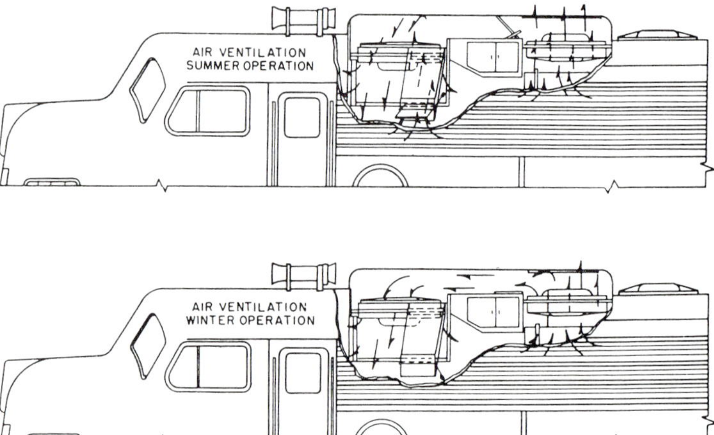

EMD E8 Engine Room Ventilating System

panels. The dirt carried by this misdirected unfiltered air contributes to plugging engine mounted air filters more rapidly, and was also ingested by the traction motor cooling blowers and the main generator blowers. The result was accumulation of dirt in the electrical equipment, tracking and flashovers, and, ultimately, road failures. Also, the draft created by the open shutter area could cause reversal of the normal engine room air circulation at high speeds, causing cool air to be drawn toward the center of the carbody, away from the main generators, thus contributing to electrical failures from overheating.

That the prime movers in the respective models were quite different contributed to the variation in arrangement of engine related accessories. (45) Changes in engine room arrangement between the 12-567B's in the E8 and the 12-567C's in the E9 were not as significant as from the 12-567A's in the E7, even though the entire crankcase and power assembly design had been vastly altered between the B and C models. As E-unit prime movers could be changed easily, it was not unusual to see an E7 or E8 equipped with 567C crankcases, or even mixtures of Cs, Bs, BCs, As, or ACs. The 567AC and 567BC hybrid models were essentially an A or B model crankcase modified to take the 567C cylinder assemblies.

Trucks on the EMD E8 and E9, as well as on E3-E7's were Blomberg A-1-A passenger locomotive trucks. This truck is an equalized design which uses equalizer arms contained in a channel in the truck main frame.

The differences between E8 and E9 locomotives were internal. The change of the prime mover from the 567B to the 567C has already been noted. Functionally, a number of refinements were made in the E9 including automatic backward transition, automatic sanding, and electrical modifications, such as the D37 traction motor replacing the D27. (45)

E-units, like all other dual engine locomotives, had a distinctive cycling vibration due to the practical impossibility of setting two prime movers at exactly the same speed. Harmonic vibration was particularly noticeable in the cab, where carbody glass and electrical cabinet doors rattled at intervals from three to ten seconds apart, depending on the difference in RPM of the prime movers. When both transmitted an impulse at the same time, the vibration increased; when the RPM difference caused one to act opposite the other, the vibration decreased. As a general rule in any two twin-engine locomotives of approximately equal power rating, the locomotive whose prime movers produce the fewest power strokes per interval seemed to have the most severe cyclic vibrations. With 12 cylinders (per engine) and one firing per cylinder per revolution, the E8 and E9 were among the smoothest of the twin prime mover locomotives. Four-cycle prime movers with fewer cylinders tended to interact much more severely.

If numbers and longevity are indicators of success, the combined E8 and E9 models qualify as two of the best passenger locomotives ever built. With many of them recording as much as six million miles of operation, they far outlived the comparable twin-engined production passenger models of other manufacturers. (39)

On the B&O

When EMD resumed E-unit production at the close of WWII with the new E7s, B&O was able to continue its dieselization program with an order of four A-units, built in February 1945. The two units were still considered a single 4,000hp locomotive, but this time the second in the pair was numbered with even numbers and an "A" suffix (instead of the "X" used on EA's and E6s), for example the first four units

were 64, 64A, 66, 66A. Four more arrived in September and ten in October 1945. In 1947 B&O resumed purchases of passenger units, but opted for 14 F3s equipped with steam generators and geared for passenger speeds, in 3-unit configurations (either ABB or ABA). Thus the resulting 4,500hp locomotive was an increase in power over the E7AA set by 500. The F3s were numbered 82, 82A, 82X, 83AX - through - 88-88x, in the passenger unit series.

But a return to the E-series was made when 17 E8A's were received: Nos. 90-90A, 92, 92-A, 94, 94-A & 96, 96A in September/October 1950. The second E8A group arrived in October/November 1953, but they were given a new series: Nos. 26, 26A, 28, 28A, 30, 30A, 32, 32A. At the same time the old EAs were traded in to EMD, and certain parts taken off of them and put on new E8s being built for the B&O. The only EA parts actually used on the new units were: main generator, auxiliary generator, batteries, radiator sections, fuel pumps and motors, load regulators, 5-chime air horn, bell and speed recorder. Because the new units used these older components, they were classified as E8Am and given a 2,000hp rating, instead of the usual 2,250 of E8s.

B&O bought four E9s, the last of the series, in May 1955: Nos. 34, 36, 38, and 40.

It should be noted that each time new locomotives were received they were fleeted down; the newest engines always assigned to the *Capitol Limited*, any that were bumped from it going to the *National Limited*, and so on until the lowest-ranked train got the oldest locomotives. All trains were gradually dieselized, though some retained steam power fairly late. By the mid-1950s the E-Units were in a general pool with no specific assignments and were used as needed.

EMD E9 - SPECIFICATIONS (EMD catalog)	
DIMENSIONS	
Length over coupler pulling faces	70' - 3"
Width over hand holds	10' - 8"
Height above rails	14' - 10 1/2"
Distance between truck centers	43' - 0"
Truck rigid wheelbase	14' - 1"
Wheel diameter	36"
Minimum curve radius	274' - 0"
SUPPLIES	
Fuel oil	1,200 gals.
Boiler water	1,350 gals.
Lubricating oil (2 engines)	330 gals.
Cooling water (2 engines)	436 gals.
Sand	18 cu. ft.
WEIGHT	
Total weight fully loaded approx.	324,800 lbs.

Baltimore & Ohio E-Unit Painting Guide

Any description of the painting and lettering of Baltimore & Ohio E-Units at this time would take exhaustive research into past literature and would not be possible on any existing locomotive. Bruce Meyer obviously did extensive research and on site measurements to come up with the information presented in his superb article "B&O E-Unit Painting Guide- A Blue and Gray Standard" which appeared in the March 1983 issue of *Mainline Modeler*. That information is presented here in its entirety. (13)

The Baltimore & Ohio blue and gray paint style for streamline diesel locomotives is perhaps the first, or at least, one of the very earliest cab unit paint schemes developed. It was first used on the 1937 "E" units and remained in use until the late 1960's. All streamlined diesels on the B&O were painted in this basic and classic style. Except for the AT&SF war bonnet scheme, the B&O style was certainly one of the best known.

The grand-daddy paint scheme used on the B&O EA's set the standard on the railroad for the next 25 years, but there were many changes to the scheme from 1937 to the end of its use in the 1960's. The EA scheme had an upper gray band followed by a blue band, then the middle black band, and finally the lower blue band. The gray anticlimber and gray pilot, with three 2-inch-wide blue stripes separated by 2 1/4 inches, were standard as long as this paint scheme was in use. All stripes on the carbody, except for a 1 3/4-inch bottom stripe, were Imitation Gold. The bottom stripe, when used, was always gray. These stripes came and went and changed location as the schemes changed over the years. The middle gold stripes on both sides of the center black band were always 1 inch wide on all variations of the scheme. Everything below the side of the carbody on all units was always the Dulux Black. The Imitation Gold road name was centered in the black band and the letters were always 5 inches tall. An ampersand was used on all early schemes, and not until the first E8's was the word "and" spelled out. The road names on the EA's, E6's, and E7's were identical. All letters and numbers were painted Imitation Gold.

One difference on the painting of EA's Nos. 51 and 52 from later schemes was the all-gray roof. Everything from just below the cooling hatch intake grills, on up and over the roof and nose, was gray. There was no gold stripe between the upper gray and first band of blue, and the center black band, with its gold stripes, was located with both gold stripes on batten strips. The bottom gray stripe was 1 3/4 inches wide at the top of the bottom batten. Beneath the gray stripe and the anticlimber and pilot, black paint was used. The front capital Medallion was a brass casting with polished

brass raised areas, black background, and an outer edge trimmed in black. The gold stripe circle around the medallion was much larger than on all following variations. Unique to the EA's was a large stainless or chrome plate on the nose, surrounding the headlight and number boards. These large curved plates came in at least two different styles. As shown on No. 51, it had two points at the sides and a long point over the top of the nose, pointed toward the center of the windows. This shiny surface on top of the nose must have reflected in the crew's eyes as later photos of the EA's show a plate with blue horizontal lines which *did not* peak over the top of the nose. This polished plate was only used on the EA's and must have made the EA's paint scheme very flashy. The unit number and class designation were located in the lower blue band, and the rear end of the EA was painted all black. The EB's were just like the EA's, including the road name, unit number, and class

Builders photograph of EA No. 52 at La Grange, Illinois, shows off the most attractive B&O paint scheme. Notice the flame design around the headlight.

designation. EA's No. 55 and No. 56 received a black roof and smaller circle around the medallion with these two changes retained on later units. They still, however, kept the stainless steel panels on the nose. From the production timing, it appears most likely that No. 53 and No. 54 had black roofs as well; however, we do not have photographs to verify that modification.

The paint scheme on the E6A's of 1940 and 1942 was only slightly changed from that of the EA's. There was no gold stripe between the black roof and the gray on any of the schemes. There was no metal plate on the nose of the E6's and the gray gently sloped down at the front under the headlight. Again, a gold stripe was not used between the gray and blue. The center black band and its gold stripes were much narrower than on the EA's. It was located by the upper gold stripe on the batten strip. The road name, unit number, and class designation were located just as on the EA's. The brass cast capitol dome was unchanged from the EA's, but the 1-inch gold stripe circle was only 2 inches from the edge of the medallion. The E6's were the only units painted with blue instead of black between the anticlimber and pilot, and under the 1 3/4-inch lower gray stripe. At least one, and maybe all of the last four E6A's were named when they were shipped from EMD. Number 62 was called "White River Junction" and the name was neatly lettered in the center of the black band in front of the front door. The letters appeared to be about 2 1/2 inches tall. The rest of the paint scheme was like that used on the

EA's, and the "B" units were painted as the "A" units.

The "modern" B&O paint scheme started with the E7A's of 1945. A 1-inch gold stripe was added between the gray and upper blue bands, located on the batten strip under the grilles. The center black band was enlarged from that used on the E6's to 16 inches wide. This width stayed standard on all following units, including non-EMD power. The area between the bottom 1 3/4-inch gray stripe and the bottom of the carbody, along with the area between the anticlimber and pilot, returned to black and remained black on the early E8's. The bumper was also black, while the anticlimber stayed gray on the E7's, as well as the following E8's. Probably due to the war, the medallion was changed to a painted 18 3/4-inch dia. 14-gauge steel plate. The striping, letters, and dome were painted standard Imitation Gold and the background was black. These medallions were undoubtedly changed to cast brass after the war. The gold circle stripe around the medallion had an inside dia. of 18 3/4 inches, the same as the outside of the medallion. Reflector number plates were added to the nose door above the B&O dome. These reflectorized numbers were used until the 1957 renumbering. The unit number and class designation was moved from under the road name to the rear of the unit. Two-inch unit numbers and 1 1/2-inch class designation letters were located 1 inch above the lower gold stripe centered between the back handholds. The addition of a unit number and class designation to the rear end of the units was a change applied to the E7's. Five-inch unit numbers, 2 inches above the 2-inch class letters, were applied 60 3/4 inches from the bottom of the carbody, centered on the right side between the door frame and side of the unit. The rest of the rear end was all black as before.

E8 locomotives were shipped to the B&O from early 1950 through the middle of 1955. The old standard B&O paint style was constantly changed during this time and up until the 1957 diesel and steam renumbering program. The 1957 B&O paint standard was then used on all streamlined diesels with only minor changes until the mid 1960's, when the all blue paint schemes came into use.

The early E8's were painted like the E7's, with about four minor changes. The medallion was again a 1/2-inch-thick brass casting with a diameter of 16 1/2 inches. However, the 1-inch gold circle stripe diameter did not change from the 18 3/4 inch diameter, which left 2 1/4 inches between the circle stripe and the medallion. The 1 3/4-inch bottom gold stripe was now above the bottom batten, with black below as on the E7. While the top gold 1-inch stripe was still located on the batten under the grilles, the middle stripes and black band were located 16 3/16 inches above the bottom of the gray stripe. Neither middle gold stripe was on a batten strip. The 5-inch road name now had "and" spelled out and was located with the "A" of the "and" 7 7/8 inches from the right middle door handhold. The "E" on "Baltimore" was located 1 inch from the left center door handhold, while the 2-inch unit numbers and now 2-inch class letters were moved forward 27 inches from the rear of the unit and placed 1 inch above the bottom stripe. The rear of the unit was different for it still had the lettering applied, as on the E7's, but the side colors wrapped around the edges of the end. The middle of the end was still black.

All of the E8's shipped in 1953 had additional changes made to the scheme. The bottom gray stripe was removed and blue was used to the bottom of the carbody. The area between the anticlimber and pilot remained black. The top gold stripe was eliminated from the front of the front door to the rear of the unit, but it remained around the front under the headlight. The 2-inch class and unit numbers at the rear of the side were now located 2 3/4 inches above the bottom batten, and center black band, with its two gold stripes, located 17 15/16 inches above the bottom batten strip.

In 1955, on the final order of E9A's the rear of the unit was again painted all black with no numbers. The 3-inch painted "F" was also replaced by a 4-inch cast "F" plate.

"E" units painted during and after 1957 had the 5-inch road name moved forward slightly so that the "A" of "and" and the "E" of "Baltimore" were centered about the center door, 5 3/4 inches from each side. The black band and its two gold stripes were now 22 inches above the bottom of the carbody. The 2-inch numbers and letters were removed from the rear side of the unit and new 5-inch unit numbers were placed 6 1/2 inches below the gold stripe, centered under the "and." One-and-one-half-inch class designations were placed two inches below the unit numbers. This unit number application was once again used as it was on the early EA's and E6's. Also, as mentioned before, the reflector numbers were removed from the front door.

(Below) Builder's photo of EMD E6A No. 57 & E6B No. 57X shows the original B&O E6 paint scheme.

EMD, Hundman Publishing Coll.

Loco Model Number	AA	EA	EB	E6A	E6B
Locomotive type	Box-cab unit	Cab unit	Booster unit	Cab unit	Booster unit
AAR Classification	B-B	A1A-A1A	A1A-A1A	A1A-A1A	A1A-A1A
Road number series	50	51-56	51X-56X	52(2),1408-1414	2407-2413
Number units	1	6	6	8	7
Engine type and mfr.	Winton 201A	Winton 201A	Winton 201A	12-567	12-567
Horsepower	1800	1800	1800	2000	2000
Gear ratio	55:22	51:25	51:25	55:22	55:22
Maximum speed, mph	98	na	na	98	98
Length, coupled, ft.-in.	64-4	71-6 3/4	70-0	71-6 3/4	70-0
Width, maximum, ft.-in.	10-0	10-6 7/8	10-6 7/8	10-6 7/8	10-6 7/8
Height above rail, ft.-in.	14-9	15-0	14-7	15-0	14-7
Total wheelbase, ft.-in.	48-6	57-1	57-1	57-1	57-1
Nominal weight, lb.	220000	287200	283000	313300	303000
Weight on drivers, lb.	220000	196000	192000	212800	205800
Starting tractive effort (25% ad.)	55000	49000	48200	52220	50500
Continuous tractive effort at mcs.	26400	16000	16000	18500	18500
Minimum continuous speed (mcs)	20	36	36	33	33
Minimum radius curve, deg.	na	21	21	21	21
Main generator model	GT535	WH-486	WH-486	EMD-D4	EMD-D4
Traction motor model	GE716C2	WH366E	WH366E	EMD-D7A	EMD-D7A
Fuel tank capacity, gal.	800	1200	1200	1200	1200
Lube oil capacity, gal.	na	250	250	220	220
Stean Gen. Capacity, lb. per hour	2000	2585	2585	2250	2250
Water tank capacity, gal.	1100	1100	1100	1050	1200
Cooling water capacity, gal.	na	na	570	570	380
Sand capacity, cubic feet	12	16	16	16	16/none

Loco Model Number	E7A	E8A	E8AM	E8BM	E9A
Locomotive type	Cab unit	Cab unit	Cab unit	Booster unit	Cab unit
AAR Classification	A1A-A1A	A1A-A1A	A1A-A1A	A1A-A1A	A1A-A1A
Road number series	1415-1432	1438-1467	1433-1437	2414-2419	1454-1457
Number units	18	24	5	6	4
Engine type and mfr.	12-567B	12-567B	12-567B	12-567B	12-567C
Horsepower	2000	2250	2000	2000	2400
Gear ratio	55:22	55:22	55:22	55:22	55:22
Maximum speed, mph	98	98	98	98	98
Length, coupled, ft.-in.	71-1 1/4	70-3	70-3	70-0	70-3
Width, maximum, ft.-in.	10-6 7/8	10-7 1/2	10-7 1/2	10-7 1/2	10-7 1/2
Height above rail, ft.-in.	14-11	14-8 7/8	14-8 7/8	14-8 7/8	14-8 7/8
Total wheelbase, ft.-in.	57-1	57-1	57-1	57-1	57-1
Nominal weight, lb.	315000	316500	329000	319000	324800
Weight on drivers, lb.	205000	210750	223400	215000	216500
Starting tractive effort (25% ad)	51250	52690	55850	53750	54100
Continuous tractive effort at mcs.	18500	23500	17600	17600	23500
Minimum continuous speed (mcs)	33	30	36	36	32
Minimum radius curve, deg.	21	21	21	21	21
Main generator model	EMD-D4	EMD-D15B	WH-486	WH-486	D15B
Traction motor model	EMD-D7A	EMD-D27B	WH-D27B	WH-D27B	D37
Fuel tank capacity, gal.	1200	1200	1200	1200	1200
Lube oil capacity, gal.	330	330	330	330	330
Stean Gen. Capacity, lb. per hour	2250	4500	2800	2880	4500
Water tank capacity, gal.	1200	1350	1950	1350	1950
Cooling water capacity, gal.	400	400	400	400	436
Sand capacity, cubic feet	16	16	16	16	18/none

E-Unit Ownership, Operation & Maintenance

B&O first did heavy (back shop type) repairs on its E-unit fleet at Mt. Clare in Baltimore, and then later at Glenwood. Running Repairs (air, oil leaks, sand pipe alignment, etc), and Running Maintenance (such as traction motor renewal, oil & air filters, flush steam generator, water & air adjustments, brake shoes, etc.) were done from 1937 until 1959 at Washington Union Terminal shops at Ivy City. WUT had a special shop force and several dedicated stalls for the B&O work. After 1959 E-unit service was done at Riverside in Baltimore, with other shops doing scheduled running maintenance, as needed.

B&O Diesel Classification System

Model	1935-40 Class	1940-57 Class	1957-64 Class
AA Box Cab	DE-1	DP-1 (note 1)	—
EA	DE-2	DP-2	—
EB	DE-2	DP-2x	—
E6A	—	DP-3	PE-2
E6B	—	DP-3x	PE-2x
E7A	—	DP-4	PE-3
E8A	—	DP-6	PE-5
E8Am	—	DP-7	PE-4
E8Bm	—	DP-7x	PE-4x (note 2)
E9A	—	DP-8	PE-6

Note 1 - When DE-1 was given its shovel nose and assigned to the Alton RR in 1937 it was reclassified DE-1x. Note 2 - E8Bm 2414 was reclassified PE-5x when upgraded to 2,250 hp in 1958.

B&O Passenger Trains Locomotive Requirements September 1965

Regular trains	35
Special trains	4
Race trains	2
Passenger helpers	2
Protect Riverside	1
Washington	1
Willard	1
Chicago	1
Cincinnati	1
Cumberland Shops	4
Riverside Shops	2
Glenwood Shops	2
Total	**56**

Passenger Locomotive Assignments, January 1967

Train	No. of units	No. of cars	Notes
1	2	12	
2	2	12	
5	3	20	
6	3	20	
7	2	14	Williard-Washington
7	1	7	Williard-Chicago
8	2	14	
9	2	14	
10	1	7	Chicago-Deshler
10	1	8	Deshler-Williard
10	2	14	Williard-Washington
11	2	14	14 cars maximum (varies)
12	2	14	14 cars maximum (varies)
19-190	1	6	
210-20	1	6	
31	1	3	Can handle 6 east of Cumberland
32	1	3	
53	2	14	
54	2	14	
57	1	7	
Race	2	14	Delaware Park

Protect: 2 - Washington; 2 - Cumberland (for helpers) ; 1 - Cumberland; 1 - Willard; 2 - Chicago; 1 - Detroit; 1 - Cincinnati;

B&O E-Unit Ownership

	EA	EB	E6A	E6B	E7	E8	E8Am	E8Bm	E9	ex-C&O E8A	Total
1937	6	6	—	—	—	—	—	—	—	—	12
1941	6	6	8	7	—	—	—	—	—	—	27
1945	5	6	8	7	18	—	—	—	—	—	44
1947	5	6	8	7	18	—	—	—	—	—	44
1950	5	6	8	7	18	8	—	—	—	—	52
1953	1	—	8	7	18	17	4	5	—	—	60
1955	—	—	8	7	18	17	5	6	4	—	65
1960	—	—	7	7	18	17	5	6	4	—	64
1965	—	—	6	6	9	17	5	6	4	—	53
1970	—	—	—	—	—	14	1	—	4	7	26

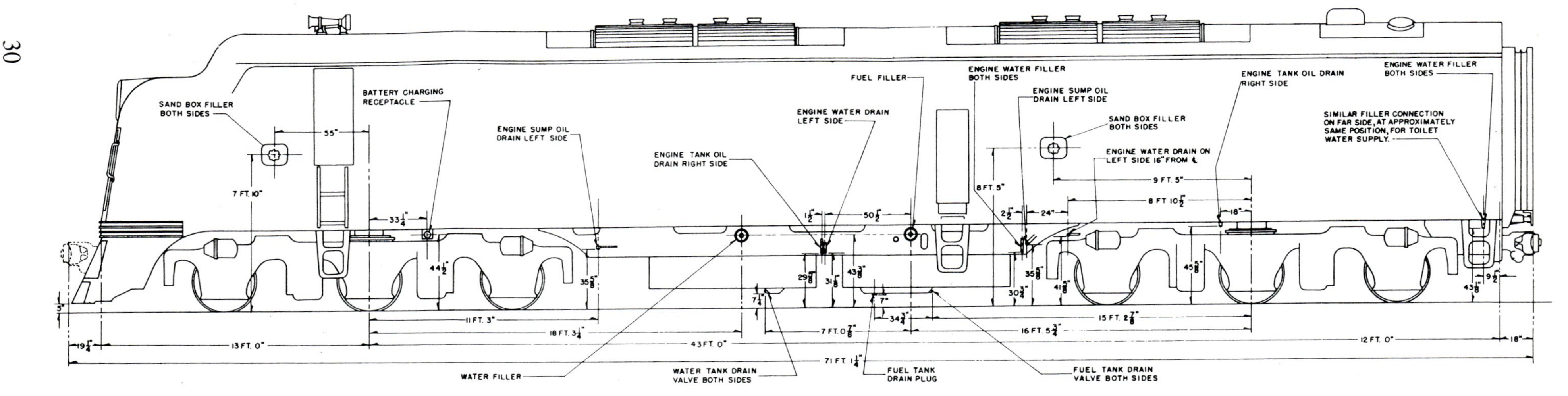

(Above) Rendering showing the paint scheme of a B&O E6 with its stylish slanted nose. (Drawn by Bob Hundman for *Mainline Modeler*—Courtesy Hundman Publishing Co).

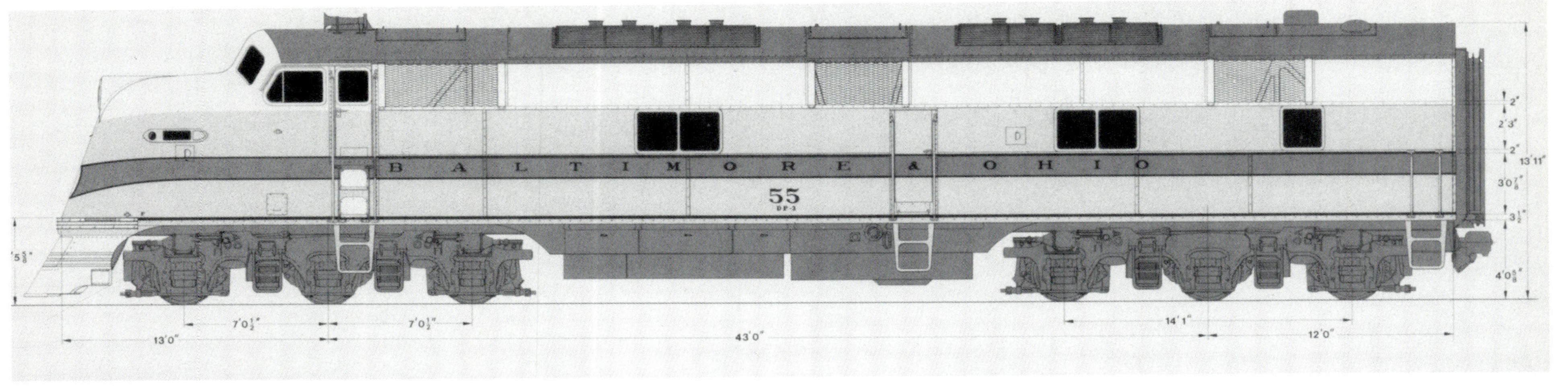

An E7A general arrangement drawing showing principal parts visible on the exterior of the body. Note the difference in the shape of the famous EMD "bulldog" style nose as compared with the steeply slanted E6 above. The E6 nose is much more in keeping with the "streamlined" styling but since there were over eight times more of the E7,8, and 9 locomotives with the bulldog nose, it is the most remembered styling. The engine exhaust manifold stacks are visible just above the location of the two prime movers.

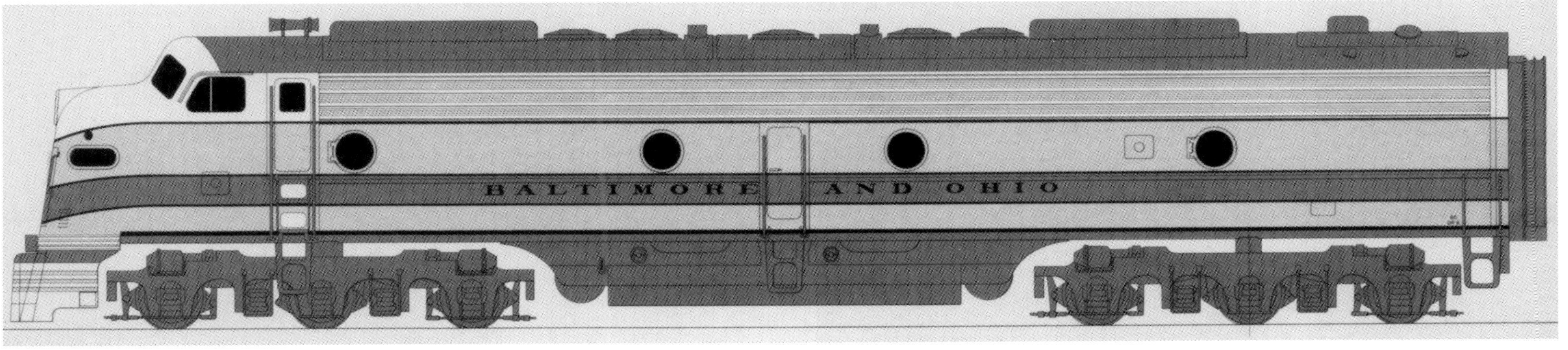

This E8A painting and lettering rendering shows the famous B&O scheme applied to the later-day units. Note the difference in the roof skyline compared with the E7 on the previous page. The engine exhaust stacks are grouped in two places and blower fans are visible around them. The portholes now replace the square windows. As Es were shopped, sometimes side panels were replaced, and thus they lost portholes. (Drawing by Bob Hundman for *Mainline Modeler* Magazine—Courtesy of Hundman Publishing Company).

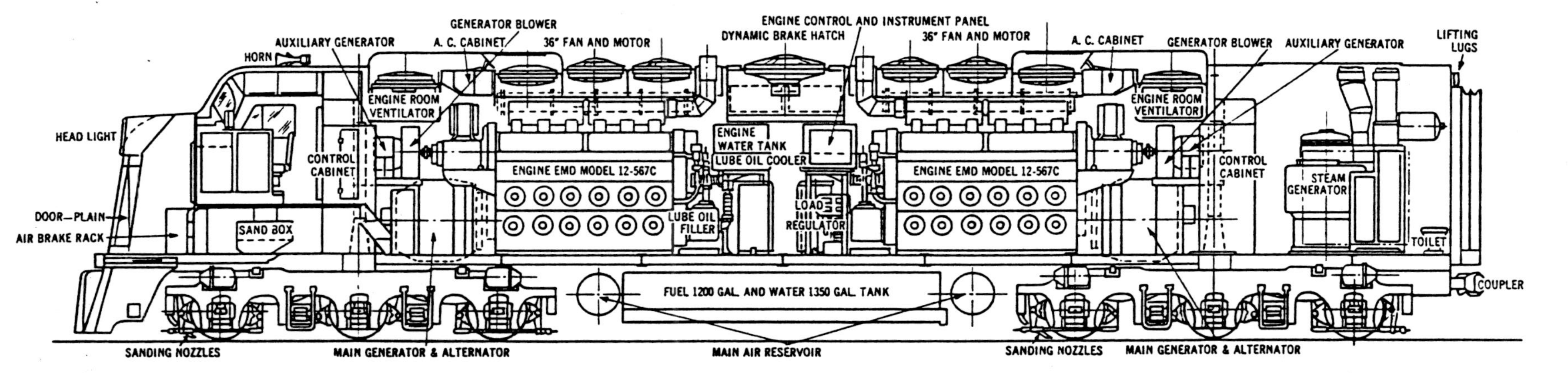

This cutaway view of an E9 shows the placement of major components and auxiliaries, including the two Model 12-567C prime movers. As you can see the two engines are set in opposite directions, a departure from previous models. The steam generator, standard on all E-units is, of course a small boiler for making steam to heat the passenger cars being hauled. Today Amtrak trains don't use steam but electrical heat. When the E-units replaced steam locomotives they were given this steam generator so that cars would not have to be modified to a new system and also could run with either type of motive power, steam or diesel. (Drawing from 1953 EMD Catalog, courtesy of William F. Howes, Jr.)

(Above) Baltimore & Ohio posed many of its trains on the Thomas Viaduct near Relay, Maryland, for publicity photos and other special events. Shown here is E9A No. 1455 with several cars not all alike. This is most likely train No. 4, *The Diplomat*. The rear car is the Louisville-Baltimore sleeper and the next to last car is St. Louis-Baltimore sleeper. *(Below)* Running along the Potomac River near Cumberland, Maryland in the fall of 1948, an E6A&B, with No. 59 in the lead, have a string of heavyweight cars in tow. The time of day would indicate that this is *The Metropolitan*.

(both) T. W. Dixon coll.

B&O E-Units in Color

E8A No. 1457 is in Washington, D. C., just recently out of the paint shop in October 1963. Although not the most attractive, this paint scheme was favored by locomotive crews because it could be seen easily at long distances. Although sometimes seen without the B&O herald on the front, the complete "sunburst" scheme included the B&O capitol dome centered in the sunburst and a yellow pilot with a dashed line along the lower edge of the carbody.

E8 No. 1451 is seen here at Detroit in October 1962, wearing the traditional B&O scheme of blue, gray and black with gold striping and lettering. It differs from the original in that the capitol dome herald has been moved from within the black stripe at the nose to above it where the Samsonite reflective numberboard was mounted until 1956.

A pair of Baltimore & Ohio E6s, headed by No. 61, are crossing the stone arch Thomas Viaduct hauling heavyweight cars in 1954. Inirially the E6s were configured to run in AB sets as a single locomotive and were numbered with the same numner, the B unit having an "X" suffix. Later in the diesel era the steam-spauned ideas of locomotives as a unit was abandoned and the concept of interchangeable "units" came into vogue. In this case two A units are running back to back.

R. Truax photo, R.R. Wallin Coll.

Baltimore & Ohio train No. 5, *The Capitol Limited*, has B&O E7A No. 66 on the point as it speeds through East Falls, Pennsylvania, on February 12, 1955.

R. R. Wallin Coll.

J. Mischke Coll.

This excellent view shows E7A No. 1423 (originally No. 72), at Detroit, in May 1961. It is coupled to an E8Bm. Note the yellow number on the nose. The large reflective Samsonite numberboards that were originally used in this location were eliminated in 1956 on all units with the large numberboards, but some of the older units had small numberboards such as this one, and in those cases the numerals were painted on the nose in yellow in the same spot that the Samonsite number plates had been used.

34

Rolling along at speed near Belle Meade, New Jersey, B&O E7A No. 78 with *The Capitol Limited* on February 20, 1955. This overhead view shows the relatively uncluttered roof of the E7s. The train itself is uniform with the modernized streamlined heavyweight cars.

(two photos) J. Mischke Coll.

(Left) EA No. 54, early in its career, leaves Jersey City, New Jersey, with Manhattan's skyline towering in the distance across the river. B&O's trains terminated in Jersey City and passengers ferried to and from Manhattan, where they were taken to and from various hotels and major buildings by B&O buses.

(Below) E6 No. 1408, wearing its blue/gray scheme, is in company of an E7B at Detroit in July 1963. Note the E8-style stainless steel grills that were fitted to E6s later in their lives.

R. R. Wallin Coll.

Harold Buckley photo, R.R. Wallin Coll.

In Silver Spring, Maryland in 1963, B&O E6A No. 1412, originally built as No. 61 in July 1941, wears fresh paint with the "sunburst" on the front surrounding the small B&O capitol herald. A yellow pilot and dashed sill stripe accent this simplified paint scheme.

J. Mischke Coll.

Outside Cumberland, Maryland, on May 31, 1966 B&O E6A No. 1413 has a B unit plus a mixture of Chesapeake & Ohio, Baltimore & Ohio, and other cars. By this time C&O and B&O had adopted the C&O yellow/blue/gray scheme for cars operating on both lines.

R.R. Wallin.

Baltimore & Ohio E7A No. 1419 waits for the next assignment with two E8Bs in the Detroit locomotive service area, in May 1961.

R. R. Wallin Coll.

E8 No. 1450 is departing St. Louis Union Station's massive trainshed in the summer of 1970. The unit is painted in the solid blue scheme with the "big B&O" lettering, and is trailing another engine painted to the C&O/B&O Blue/gray standard. There has been a collision of some tye causing dents to the right side of the nose.

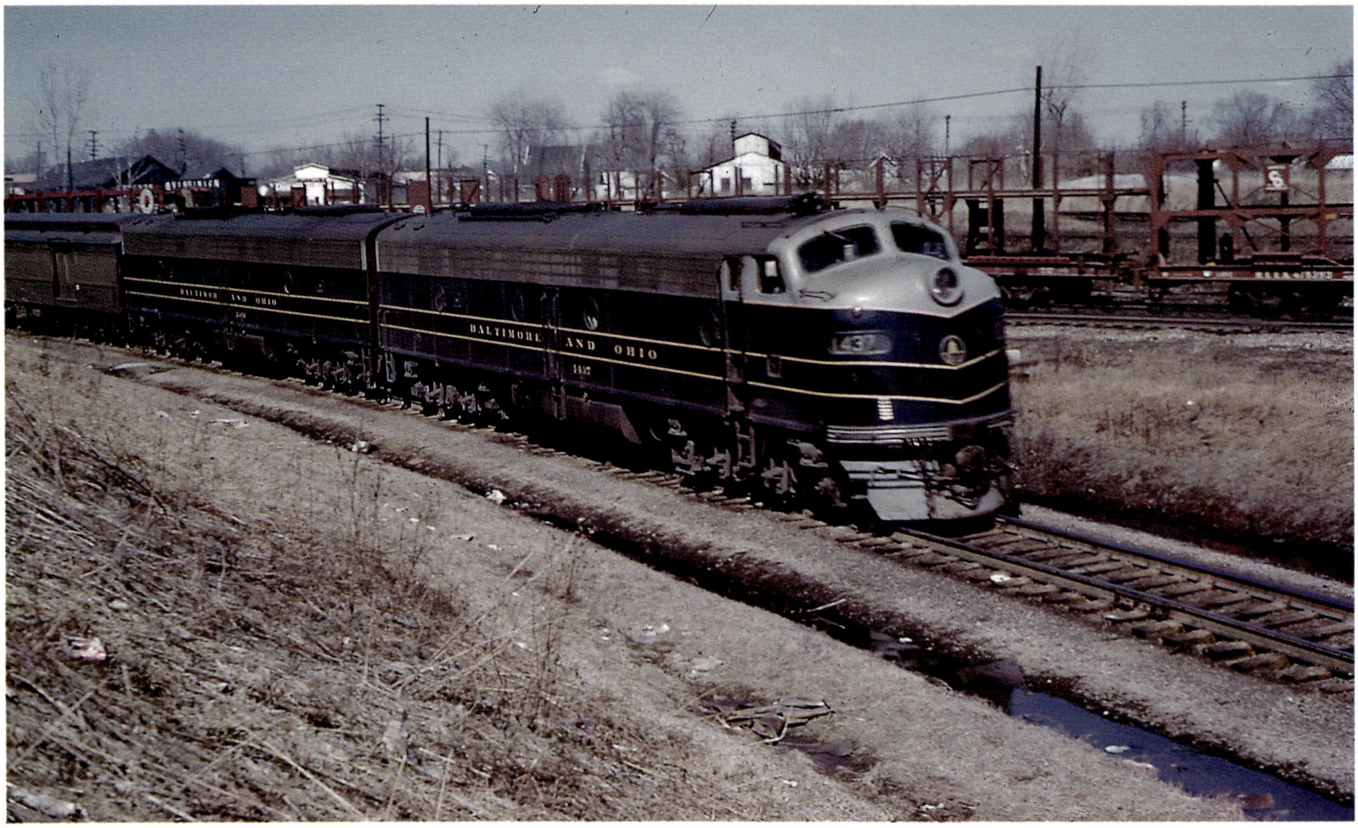
R.R. Wallin collection.

In June 1962, B&O E8Am No. 1437 waits with an E8Bm for the train preparation in Toledo, Ohio. The EA and EB units of 1937 were traded in to EMD in 1953-54 and some parts were used in construction of E8s. The E8Am and E8Bm resulted, with 2,000hp rating because of their use of the salvaged parts, the "m" indicating a rebuild.

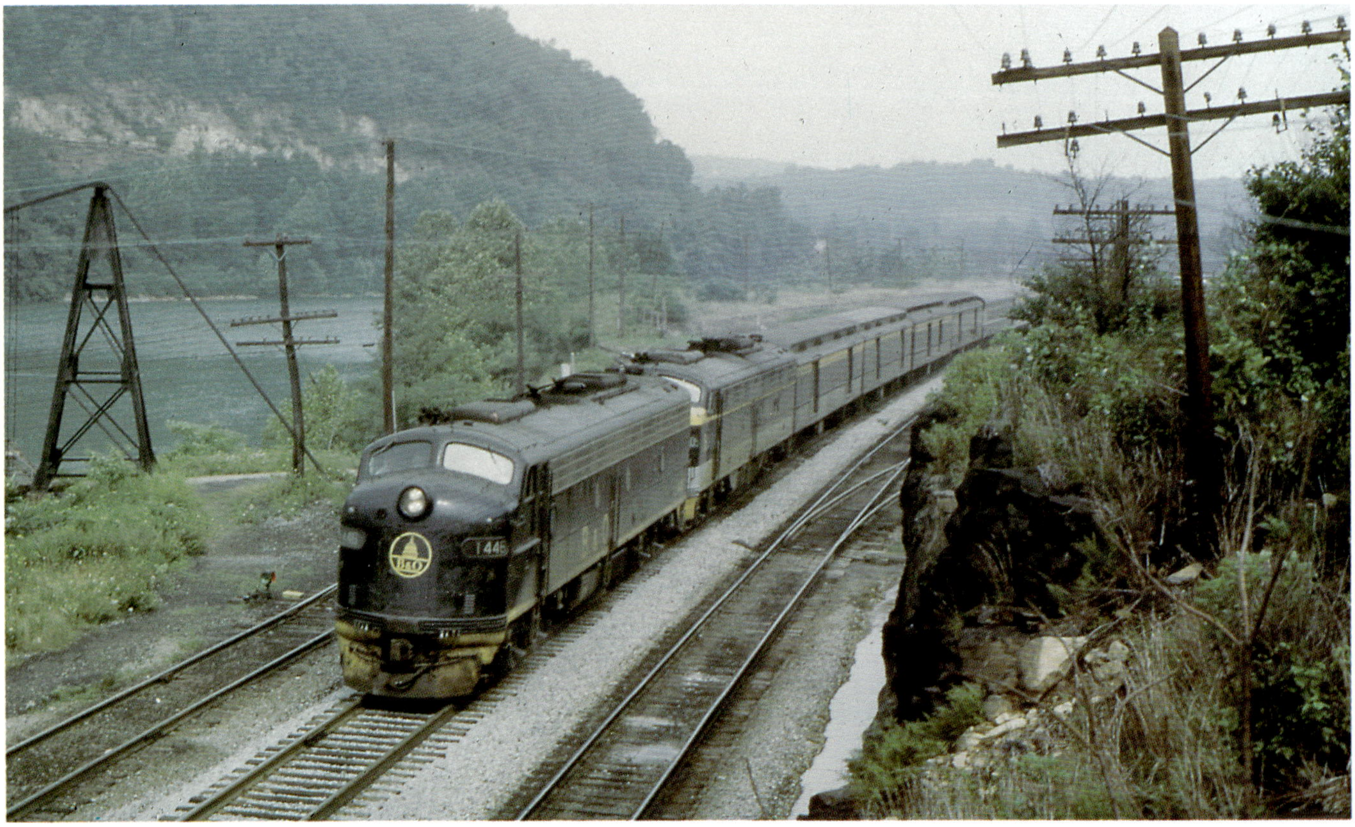
J. Mischke Coll.

On an overcast and partly cloudy day near Connelsville, Pennsylvania, on August 22, 1970, B&O E8A No. 1446 wears solid blue paint with minimal yellow trim as it heads west with a C&O E8A trailing a mail/express train consisting of four C&O and B&O head-end cars.

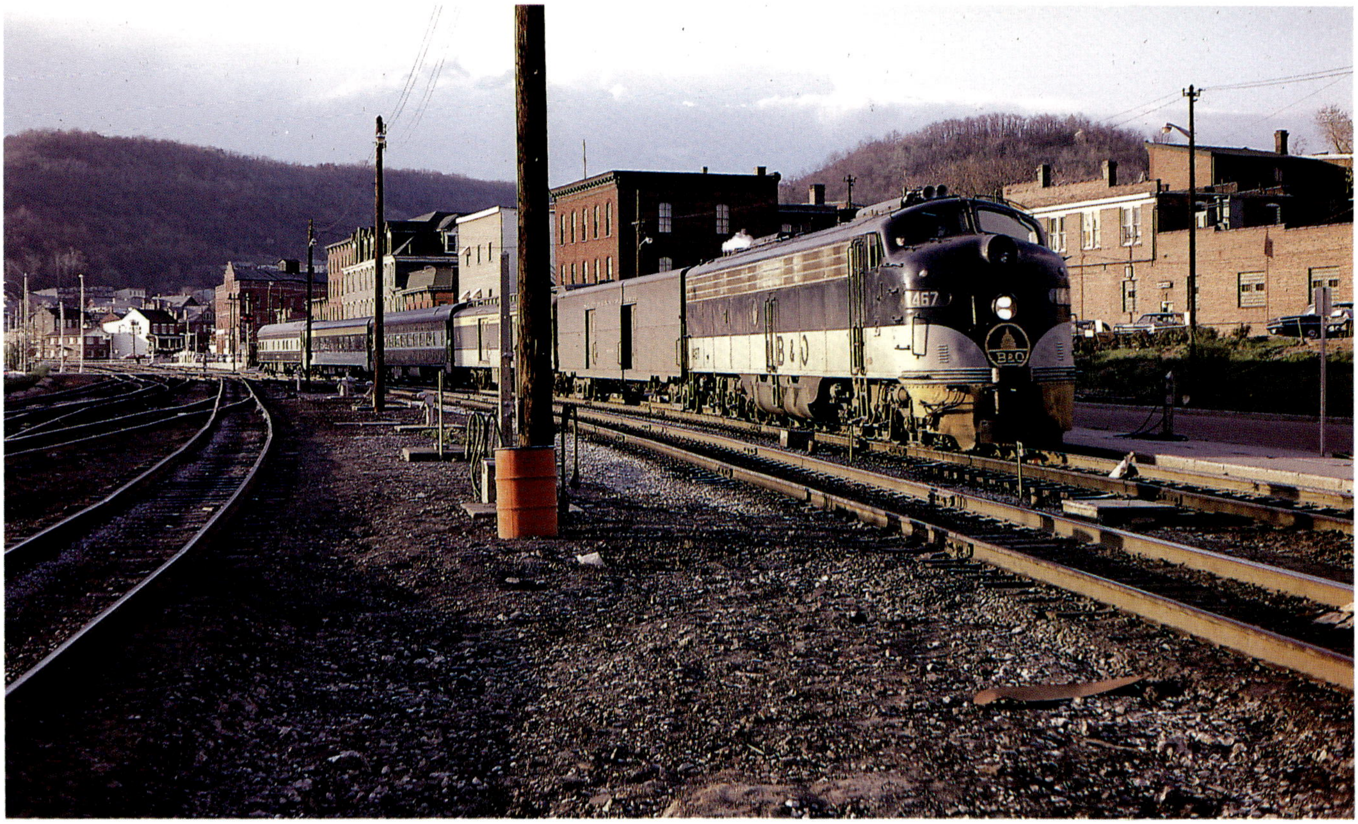

Tom Biery

Baltimore & Ohio's *Metropolitan* eases toward the station in Cumberland, Maryland, in the late afternoon in May 1970. B&O E8A No. 1467 was formerly Chesapeake & Ohio E8A No. 4013, built in November 1951, and transferred to B&O ownership in 1967. Former C&O units were distinguishable by the second headlight in the nose door.

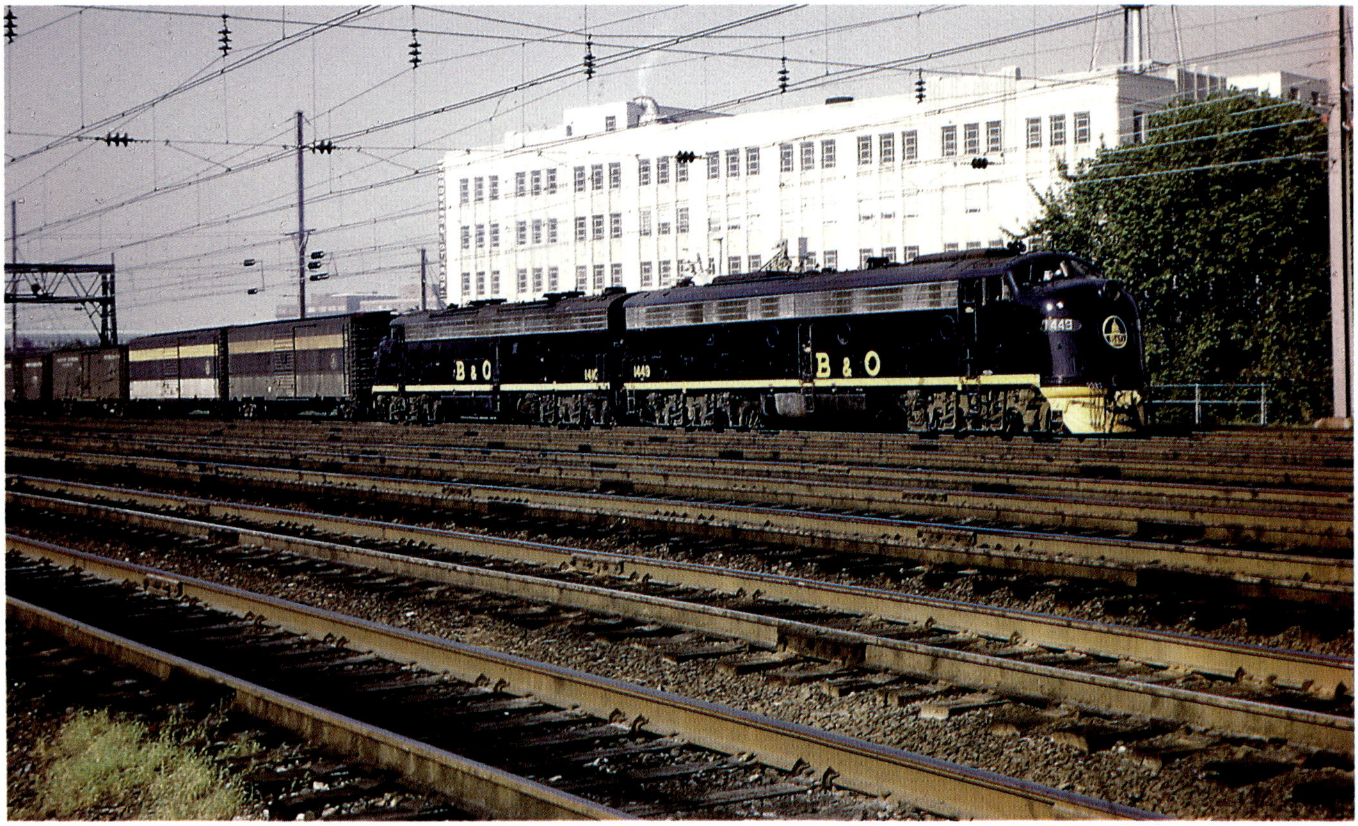

Marlo Industries, R.R. Wallin Coll.

Departing Washington Union Station on May 21, 1966, B&O E8A 1449 and E6A No. 1410 ease out under the catenary wire. Both units are fresh in their simplified all-blue with yellow lettering.

Dressed in the original blue and gray scheme, with gold striping, Baltimore & Ohio E8A No. 1451 is in Detroit, Michigan, in June 1961.

Louis A. Marre

On August 30, 1968, Baltimore & Ohio ran a special train out of Camden Station in Baltimore headed by E8A No. 1451. Showing signs of missle damage on the nose, the unit is nevertheless in good paint with the yellow pilot and lettering still bright.

Charlie Houser, J. Mischke Coll.

B&O E9A No. 1454, the first of B&O's E9s, waits to leave Grand Central Station in Chicago on May 31, 1964. The paint scheme is without a sunburst, only a small herald on the nose, illustrating how many variations there were to the many different paint schemes applied to the E-units, especially in the last ten years of their operation.

R.R. Wallin.

In Baltimore on April 29, 1971, B&O E8A No. 1461 (ex-C&O 4011) and C&O E8A No. 1471 are ready to depart Camden Station with the last run of *The Capitol Limited.* Some C&O E7s and E8s were renumbered into the B&O 1400-series but were never transferred in ownership so retained their C&O markings even though their service was almost exclusively on the B&O.

J. Mischke Coll.

Tom Biery

Eastbound out of Cumberland, Maryland, in August 1970,only a few months before Amtrak, B&O's *Metropolitan* rolls past Mexico tower with only one coach and three head end cars behind E9A No. 1455 in the standard C&O/B&O blue/gray scheme..

Douglas B. Nuckles

Amtrak E8 No. 200 leads *The Potomac Special* on the B&O at Harpers Ferry, West Virginia, on June 1, 1972. No. 200 was B&O 1439 (originally No. 90), built in September 1950. It was one of 11 B&O E8s and four E9s that were transferred to Amtrak to serve out their last four or five years of life until Amtrak got enough new locomotives.

EA Photo Section

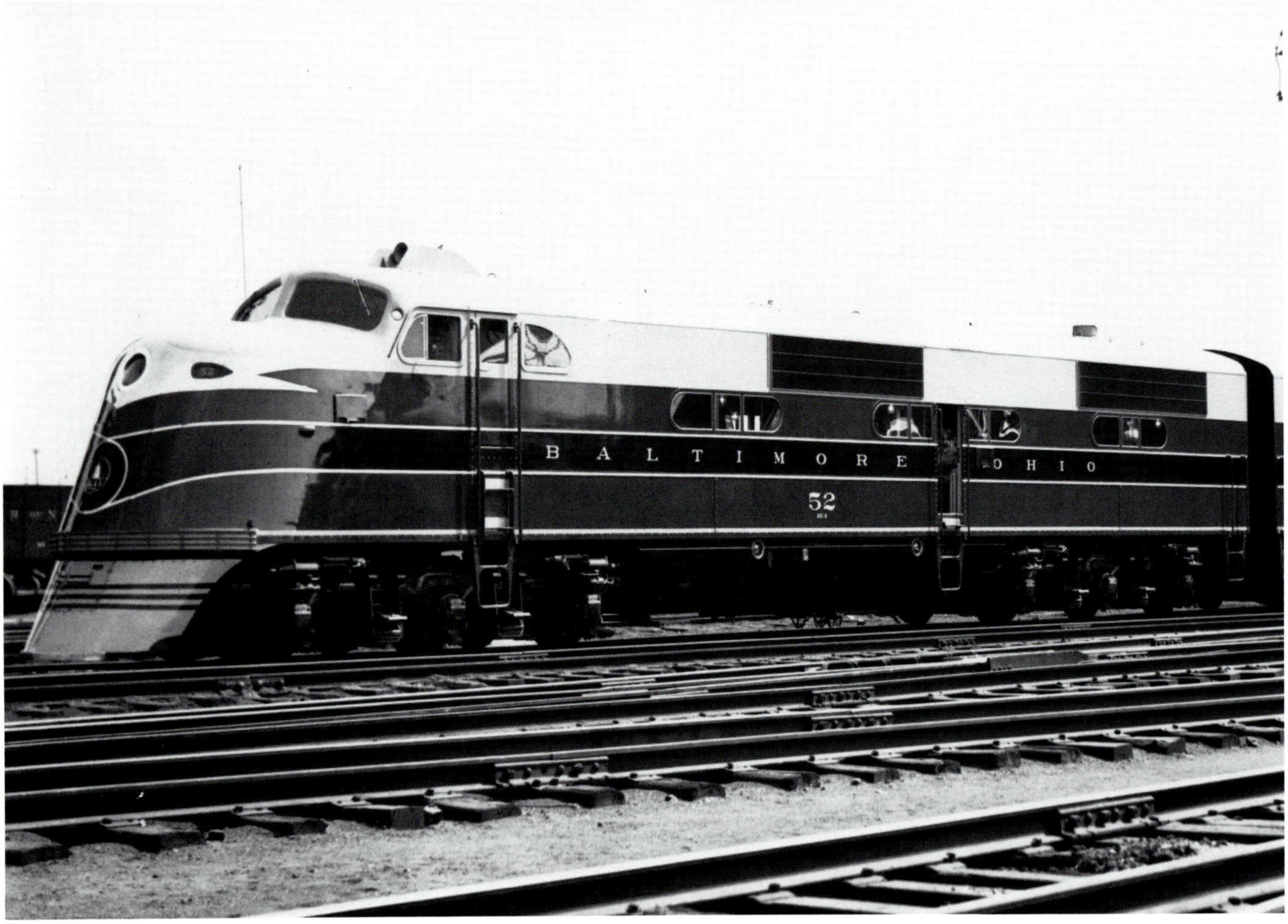

B. R. Meyer Coll.

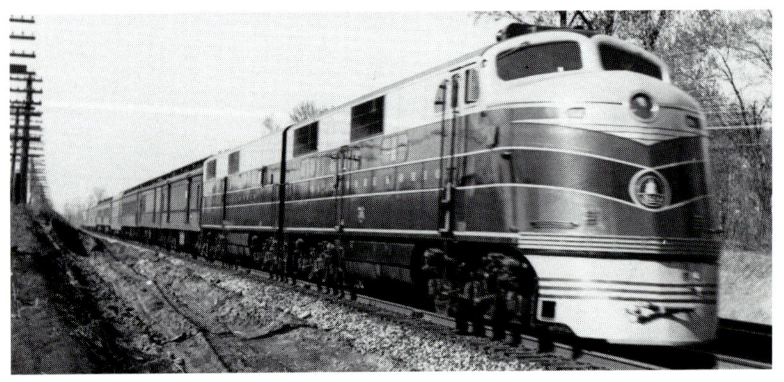

In Communipaw, New Jersey, on June 17, 1939, EA No. 52 is ready to head back to Washington, D.C. from Jersey City in B&O's "New York" service. This is another excellent example of the blue and gray classic paint scheme.

B&O RR Historical Society

B&O train No. 2, *The National Limited*, headed by EA No. 56, races through Holmes, Pennsylvania, on April 1, 1945, with a consist of standard heavyweights and modernized cars intermingled, and wearing the second paint scheme, stripes instead of the flame design around the headlight.

EA Model — 1800 hp, Class DP-2 (1940-1957)

Road No.	Second Road No.	EMD Constr No.	Date Built	Disposition
50(2nd)	52(1st)	668	6/37	renumbered 50(2nd) and transferred to then subsidiary Alton RR, renumbered 100A 1943, went to GM&O E8Am No. 100A(2nd) 1953.
51(1st)	-	666	5/37	donated less main generator and some parts to B&O RR Museum.
53(1st)	-	765	1/38	*
54(1st)	-	766	1/38	*
55(1st)	-	767	6/38	*
56(1st)	-	800	6/38	*

* Traded in to EMD with some parts used on E8Am's in 1953 and 1954.

The Capitol Limited, with EA No. 52/52X, is backing into Washington Union Station under a pair of signal bridges in 1938.

Nos. 52 and 52X having dropped their train at Union Station are moving to the Ivy City service area in Washington, D. C. in September 1938.

L. W. Rice, H. H. Harwood, Jr. Coll.

EB Model — 1800 hp, Class DP-2 (1940-1957)

Road No.	Second Road No.	EMD Constr No.	Date Built	Disposition
(51)	51X(lst)	667	5/37	
(52)	52X(lst)	669	6/37	B&O EB units originally shared a number with the EA mate unit; renumbered with an "X" after the number in 1947, then renumbered as "B" units in 1948; renumbered back to "X" units in 1952; traded in on E8Bm units in 1953-54.
(53)	53X(lst)	768	1/38	
(54)	54X(lst)	769	1/38	
(55)	55X(lst)	770	6/38	
(56)	56X(lst)	801	6/38	

John Krause, T. W. Dixon Coll.

In the 1940s the flame scheme around the headlight gave way to a striped modification. EA No. 54 is running through Fanwood, New Jersey, in A-B combination in February 1947.

L. W. Rice, T. W. Dixon Coll.

(Above) On the front service tracks at Ivy City Engine Terminal in Washington, D. C., almost new EA No. 52 pauses under a fueling tower. Note the clean lines and the shape of the pilot which was altered somewhat when it was rebuilt. Both the flame scheme and the slightly recessed headlight are noticeable in this July 2, 1937 photo.

(Right) Stopped in Parkersburg, West Virginia, one of the crew climbs down to make an inspection. EA No. 56 has the B-unit plus a steam locomotive as a helper on this day.

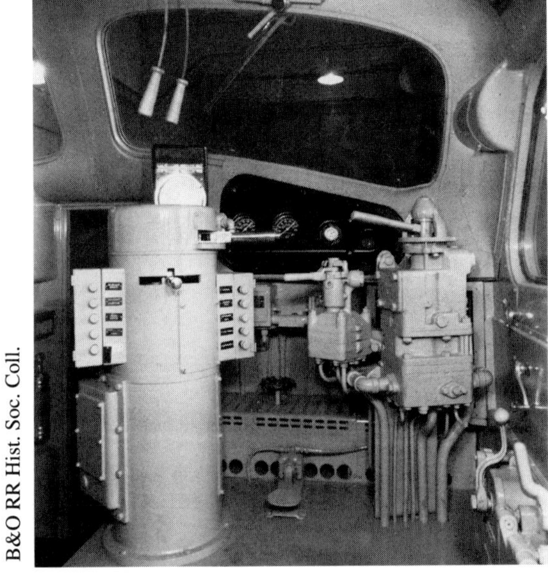

B&O RR Hist. Soc. Coll.

(Above) Engineer's controls on an EA (with seat removed).

Louis. A. Marre Coll.

L. W. Rice, H. H. Harwood Jr. Coll.

L. W. Rice, T. W. Dixon Coll.

(Above) At Ivy City Engine Terminal in Washington, D.C., in December 1946, B&O EA&B 55 and 55X are recently arrived and ready for service before the next trip.

(Left) The "B" units were rarely photographed alone. Here is 51B, class DP-2X, was found standing alone in Ivy City in December 1946.

R. H. Kennedy, Louis A. Marre Coll.

On March 26, 1938 EA No. 52 is leaving Chicago with *The Capitol Limited.* In this view the "flame" around the headlight is very plain. The nine-car train is all standard clerestory-roof heavyweight equipment.

EMD, Hundman Publishing Coll.

Builder photo of EA/EB set No. 51 new at the EMD La Grange plant in 1937, shows very clearly the first paint scheme with its "flame" around the recessed headlight and the pointed pilot. Note also that the air horns have fins to each side of them.

B. R. Meyer, Hundman Publishing Coll.

By comparison, here is EA No. 51 on display in the B&O Railroad Museum in Baltimore. It is painted in a scheme very much similar to the original EA scheme. There are exceptions which should be noted: 1) The roof is black. 2) There are no stripes on the pilot. 3) There is no lower gray stripe along the bottom edge of the body. 4) It has a gold stripe between upper gray and blue which was not in use in 1937. 5) There are no unit number or class letters on the sides. The pilot is a more modern version than that used on the EAs. There is no chrome or stainless nose plate. This unit was one of the group which was traded in to EMD in 1953 for salvage parts to be used on E8Am's. The company had established the B&O Museum at about that time, and made a donation of one of the units after the reusable parts were taken off for use on the new locomotives.

E6 Photo Section

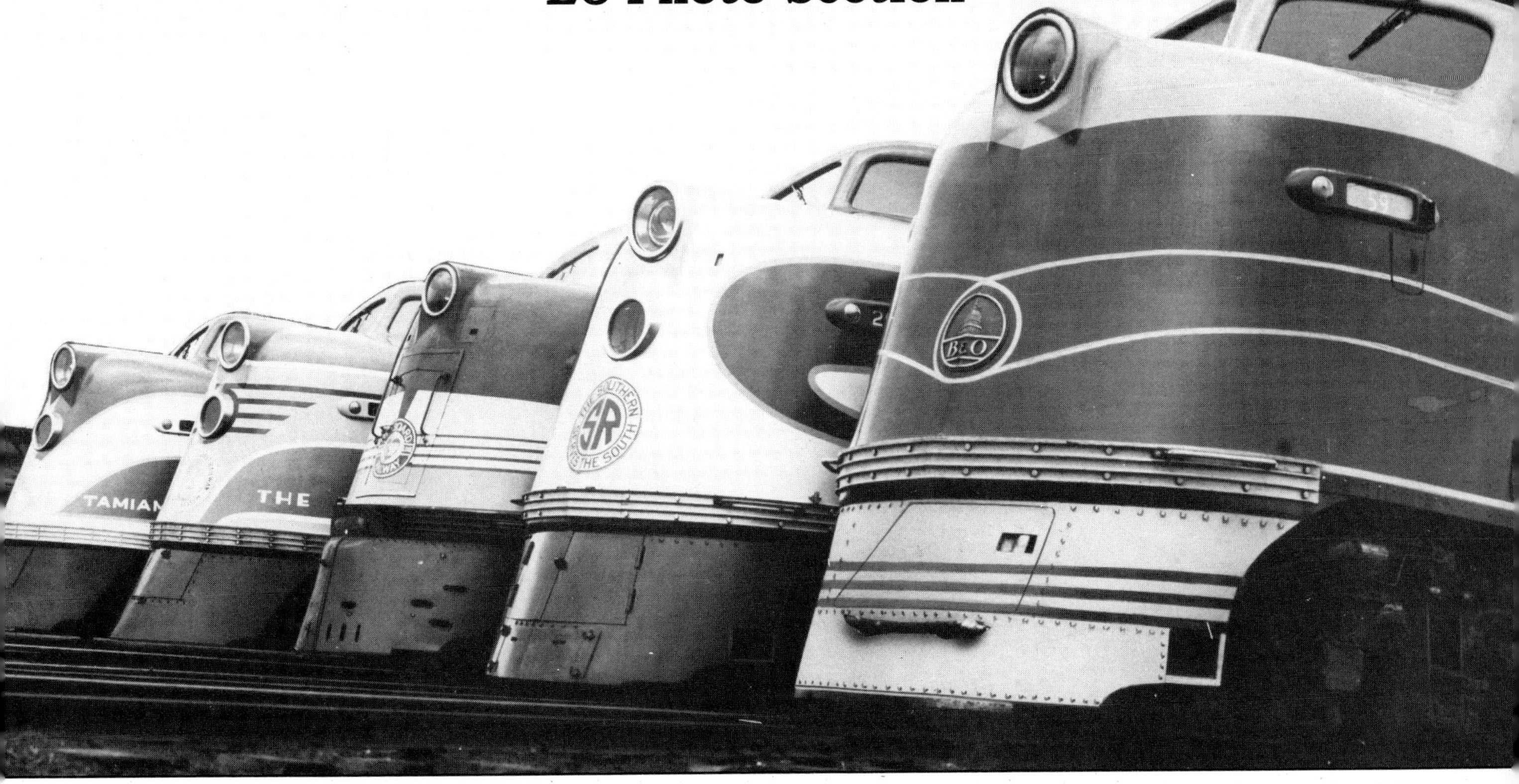

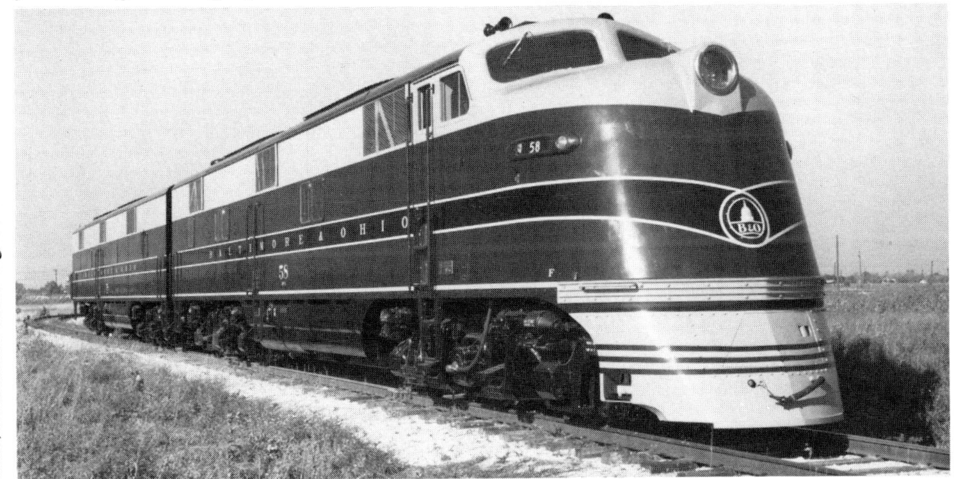

T. W. Dixon Coll.

In an EMD publicity photo circa 1940, no less than 5 E6As are lined up. With B&O No. 59 the most prominent. The others belong to connecting railroads through Washington, D. C. The first truly mass production E-Unit, the E6 model quickly found favor with many railroads. The E6 was distinguished by its slant nose design and was visibly different in front with its protruding headlight, not found on the EAs.

EMD, Hundman Publishing Coll.

E6 No. 58 is in fresh paint at La Grange, Illinois. This view shows the slanted nose and pilot along with the protruding headlight not found on the EAs.

E6A Model — 2000 hp, Class DP-3

Road No.	Second Road No.	EMD Constr No.	Date Built	Disposition
52(2nd)		1094	10/40	wrecked and scrapped, 1956.*
57	1408	1091	9/40	scrapped in 1968 at Naporano Iron & Metal.
58	1409	1092	9/40	traded in to EMD on SD40 order in 1967.
59	1410	1093	9/40	scrapped in 1968 at Naporano Iron & Metal.
60	1411	1328	6/41	traded in to EMD on SD40 order in 1967.
61	1412	1329	7/41	scrapped in 1968 at Naporano Iron & Metal.
62	1413	1330	7/41	scrapped in 1968 at Naporano Iron & Metal.
63	1414	1331	7/41	scrapped, 1962.

* wrecked at Cornwallis, W.VA., would have been renumbered 1407

The great length of E6A&B units is obvious in this EMD posed scene at La Grange, Illinois, in 1941. The only B&O locomotive ever named, E6 No. 62 was lettered *White River Junction*. Daniel Willard, president of Baltimore & Ohio from 1910 to 1941, was born near White River Junction, Vermont, and after his death in 1942, was laid to rest near there.

(both) EMD Photo, Hundman Publishing Coll.

(Above) Front view of E6A No. 62 showing the prominent headlight and the clean sloping pilot with retractable coupler pocket closed. *(Above, right)* Rear view of E6B No. 62, class DP-3X, showing the details on the rear of the unit. Both views are builder photos by EMD at at La Grange, Illinois, in June 1941.

The only named Baltimore & Ohio E-Unit was E6A No. 62, adorned with the name *White River Junction* when it was delivered in 1941. A photograph of this locomotive appeared in the September 1941 issue of the *Electro-Motive Division Instruction Manual for the Operation of E6 locomotives Nos. 60-63.* No. 62, was named in honor of long-time B&O president Daniel Willard just a year before his retirement. Upon his death in 1942 he was returned by rail to White River Junction, Vermont, a short distance from his birthplace.

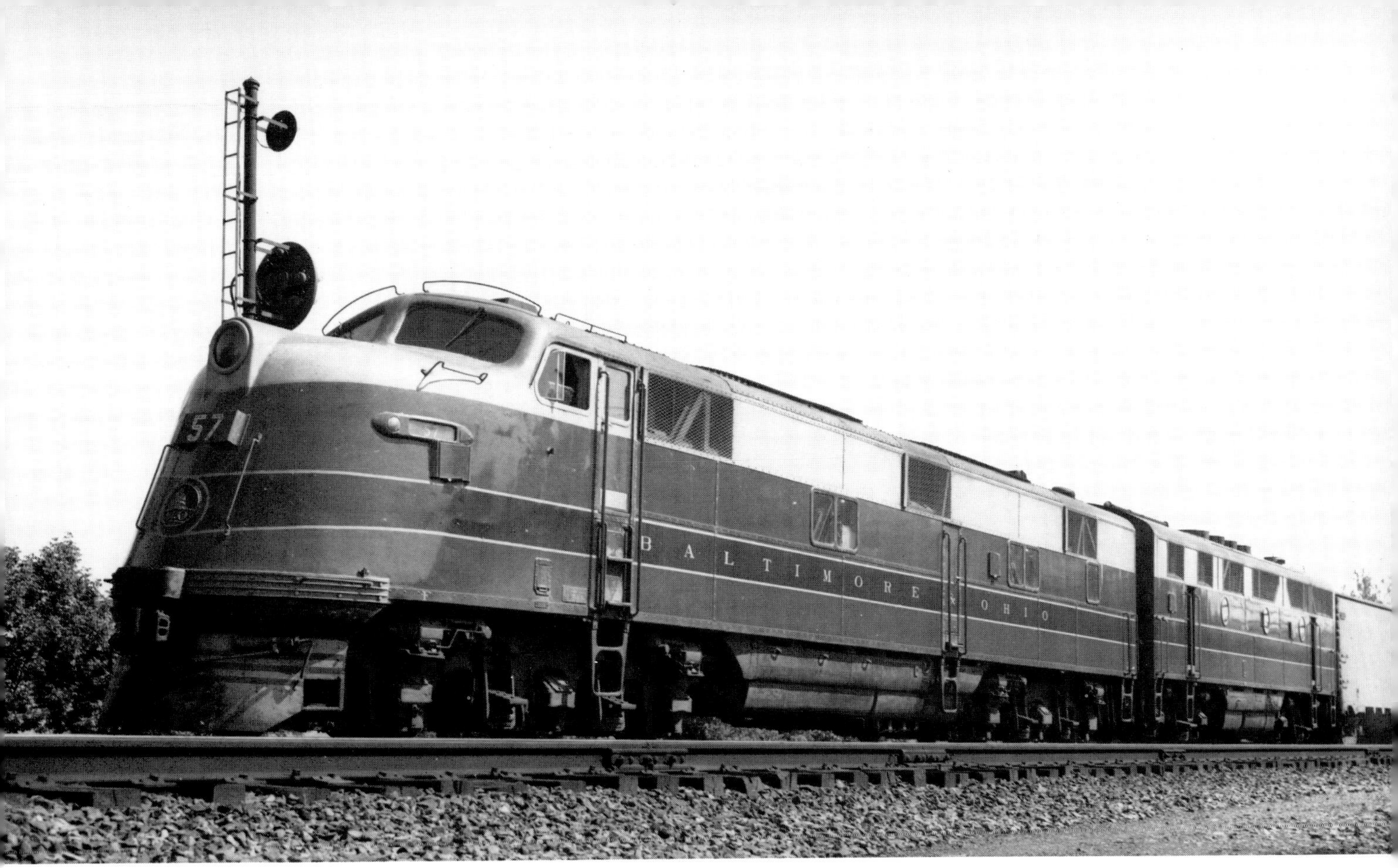

An E6A and E7B at Laurel, Maryland, on July 16, 1954. At first glace it may seem to be on a feight train, but that's an express refrigerator car of some typedirectly behind it.—Note the newer “freight style' pilot. Paul Dunn, T. W. Dixon Coll.

Richard J. Cook, Sr.

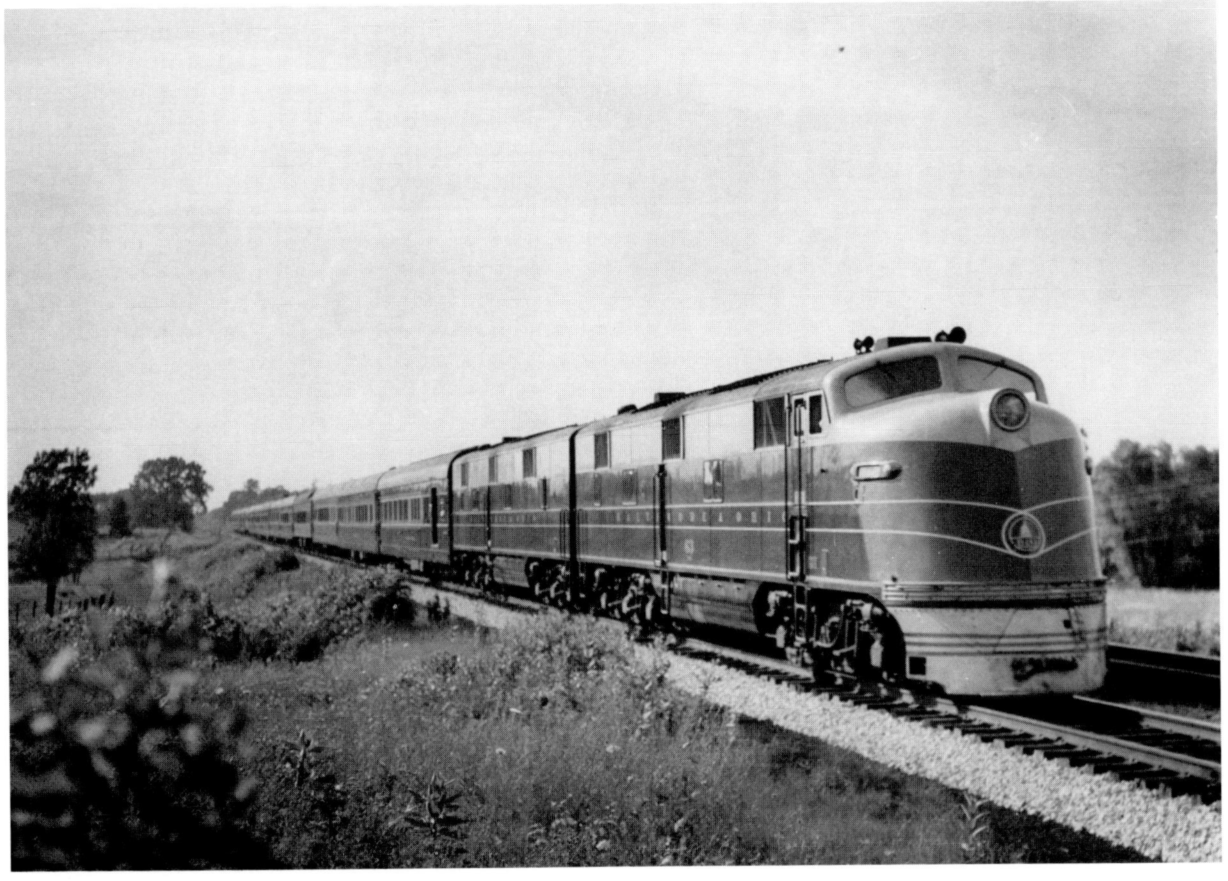

The Capitol Limited, train No. 6, is running about 60 miles per hour eastbound near Woodvale, Indiana, on June 29, 1942, with 12 cars and a set of E6AB for power.

EMD, Hundman Publishing Coll.

Brand new at La Grange, Illinois, E6A&B No. 57 pose for builder's photographs in May 1940. As delivered the locomotives did not have the large Samsonite reflective numbers later attached on brackets by B&O shop forces to aid in identifying the unit number to tower operators along the line since the early E-units had such small numberboards. During E7 production this was modified by EMD and eliminated the need for railroads to add additional indetifying marks.

T. W. Dixon Coll.

B&O RR Hist. Soc. Coll.

(Above) Rebuilt E6A No. 60 is with a passenger train at Wilmington, Delaware, on May 5, 1956. Note the modified pilot, the E8 style grills, and only one porthole on this side.

(Right) Hostler's station in an E6B. So that B-units could be moves about separately at engine terminals the E6B's were equipped with a simplified control station near the rear side window (which could be opened for forward/rear view.

H. H. Harwood, Jr.

In Riverside Yard in Baltimore, rebuilt E6A No. 1411 is paired with E9A No. 1457. The steam generator in the E9 is popping off. Notice that the E6 only has one porthole left, and the E9 has already lost one to new sheet metal work.

Louis A. Marre Coll.

On December 3, 1966 *The National Limited* is ready to leave Cincinnati Union Terminal with a pair of rebuilt E6As in the all-blue paint scheme.

(Above) B&O train No. 7, with 13 cars, is near Lodi, Ohio, in April 1957. E6A No. 1409 is leading, followed by an E7A. *(Right)* B&O rebuilt E6A No. 1411 with an E7A in Washington, D.C., in a near perfect view of the lead locomotive. *(Below)* E6A No. 1413, coupled to an E8A, sits on the service track at Riverside Yard, Baltimore, in February 1965.

Jim Shaw, Hundman Publishing Coll.

H. H. Harwood, Jr.

In the hamlet of Magnolia, West Virginia, B&O train No. 11, *The Metropolitan Special,* rolls north under the viaduct on October 30, 1952, behind a pair of E6As led by No. 63. Scenes such as this call up memories of the early development of the B&O through the east central states.

William P. Price

EMD, Hundman Publishing Coll.

Even in a front view the sloping nose of an E6A is imposing and stands out prominently. This view provides a good view of the Baltimore & Ohio capitol dome brass medallion used on the nose in earlier days.

E6B Model — 2000 hp, Class DP-3X

Road No.	Second Road No.	EMD Constr No.	Date Built	Disposition
57X	2407	1095	9/40	scrapped in 1968 at Naporano Iron & Metal.
58X	2408	1096	9/40	scrapped in 1968 at Naporano Iron & Metal.
59X	2409	1097	9/40	scrapped in 1968 at Naporano Iron & Metal.
60X	2410	1332	6/41	sold for parts to L&N 10/66, scrapped.
61X	2411	1333	7/41	trade-in on 1964 SD35 order.
62X	2412	1334	7/41	trade-in on 1967 SD40 order.
63X	2413	1335	7/41	trade-in on 1967 SD40 order.

E7 Photo Section

Louis A. Marre Coll.

B&O E7A No. 70 idles at Cumberland, Maryland, while the crew of a westbound train makes ready to depart. This is a classic pose for an E-unit with almost perfect lighting for photography. An attentive railfan or employee sits in a chair closely observing the action this warm summer day, June 4, 1949. Interesting background in this photo includes a steel girder arrangement with penstocks for watering steam locomotives stopped on passenger trains, and the impressive facade of the Queen City Hotel/depot, long a landmark here.

E7A Model, 2000 hp, Class DP-4

Road No.	Second Road No.	EMD Constr No.	Date Built	Disposition
64	1415	1673	2/45	to EMD on SD40, 1966.
64A	1416	1674	2/45	sold for scrap, Naporano Iron & Metal, 1968.
66	1417	1675	2/45	to EMD on GP35, 1964.
66A	1418	1676	2/45	to EMD on GP35, 1964.
68	1419	2897	9/45	to EMD on SD35, 1964.
68A	1420	2898	9/45	sold for scrap, Naporano Iron & Metal, 1968.
70	1421	2899	9/45	sold for scrap, Naporano Iron & Metal, 1968.
70A	1422	2900	9/45	to EMD on SD35, 1965.
72	1423	2901	10/45	sold for scrap, Naporano Iron & Metal, 1968.
72A	1424	2902	10/45	sold for scrap, Naporano Iron & Metal, 1968.
74	1425	2903	10/45	to EMD on SD40, 1966.
74A	1426	2904	10/45	sold for scrap, Naporano Iron & Metal, 1968.
76	1427	2905	10/45	to EMD on SD35, 1964.
76A	1428	2906	10/45	to EMD on SD35, 1964.
78	1429	2907	10/45	to EMD on SD35, 1964.
78A	1430	2908	10/45	to EMD on SD40, 1966.
80	1431	2909	10/45	scrapped, 1962.
80A	1432	2910	10/45	scrapped, 1962.

(Above) *The Metropolitan Special* approaches Bond, Maryland, on March 10, 195,1 behind B&O E7A No. 79 with a B-unit trailing. It's easy to see why B&O added the large numbers on the front of their E-units since this is taken from a tower operator's perspective and the small numberboards facing sideways would certainly be hard to read as a train went by at speed while handing up orders!   William P. Price

(Right) Idling with steam showing at the pilot, next to two water towers from the steam era, B&O E7A No. 72 is shining with fresh paint at Ivy City Engine Terminal in Washington, D. C., in February 1946.

(both) Louis A. Marre Coll.

A 3/4 roster view of B&O E7A in the original paint scheme at Athens, Ohio, on May 30, 1953. In this photo the vertical grills behind the cab door, a distinctive E7 feature, are very visible.

The westbound mail/express train No. 31 passes Attica Junction, Ohio in July 1956, with E7A No. 64 in the lead with an E8A trailing, typical of action along the railroad in the great passenger train era.

(both) H. H. Harwood, Jr.

The old shops at Martinsburg, West Virginia, are shown behind *The National Limited* westbound with E7A No. 1416 on the point in June 1963. Note that this is a rebuilt E7 which has E8 style grills as well as other modifications.

(Above) B&O train No. 101, the westbound *National Limited* with the last 3-car consist, is leaving Camden Station in Baltimore in August 1966 with E7A No. 1426. Note the observation car on the rear.

H. H. Harwood, Jr.

(Left) At Willard, Ohio, named for former B&O president Daniel Willard, E7A No. 1427 and an E8B unit power a train heavy with head end traffic. Note the sunburst scheme on the nose of the lead unit, but without the B&O capitol dome herald.

Louis A. Marre

(Below) This broadside view of E7A No. 1424 is at Riverside Yard in Baltimore, in November 1967. This unit has obviously seen a lot of service; notice the open shutters on the roof.

H. H. Harwood, Jr.

H. H. Harwood, Jr.

(Above) B&O E7A No. 1423 is at Chicago, in September 1967. This may be the only B&O E-unit to have the road number under the cab window, seen here in the solid blue scheme with solid stripe and nose herald, in September 1965.

(Right) Backing into Grand Central Station in Chicago, in October 1963, is E7A No. 1428 with an E8A. Notice the sunburst paint scheme on the E7 complete with the B&O Capitol herald.

Louis A. Marre

H. H. Harwood, Jr.

B&O E7A No. 1421 and E8B westbound with train No. 7, the *Diplomat*, leaving Akron, Ohio station in October 1967. The train is entirely composed of cars painted to the C&O scheme.

In a classic 3/4 roster shot, B&O E7A No. 1429 is in the company of an E8A at Clarksburg, West Virginia, in June 1957. This unit was modified or rebuilt within the next two years. This view offers a good look at the famous "chicken wire" grills on the E7s, and constrasts them with the much more pleasing stailness steel ones on the following E8.

F. R. Kern, Jay Potter Coll.

The eastbound *Capitol Limited* at Washington, D. C. in April 1959 with E7A No. 1429, which was modified by the B&O with no windows and a later style grill and F-unit number light boards.

B. R. Meyer, Hundman Publishing Coll.

A four unit set of E-units are leaving Camden Station in Baltimore with the westbound *Capitol Limited* in July 1965. Note the number under the cab window; this is thought to be the only unit so lettered.

H. H. Harwood, Jr.

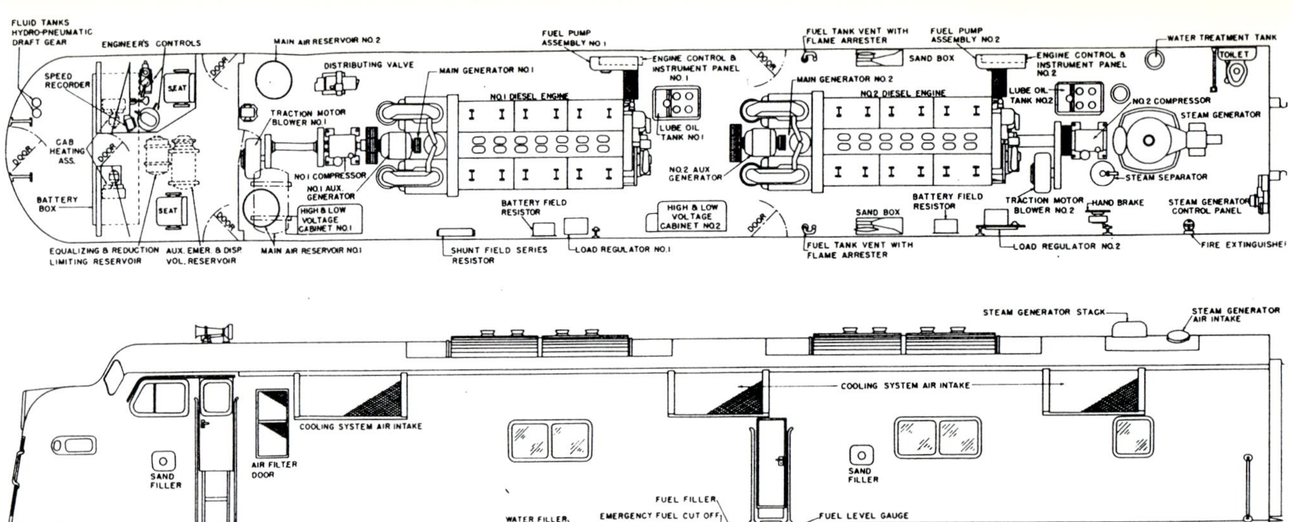

EMD Operating Manual

Diagrams of the general arrangement of parts and equipment for E7A units.

HYDRO-PNEUMATIC RETRACTABLE DRAFT GEAR

The front draft gear and coupler are hydro-pneumatically operated with the air pressure supplied to the hydraulic fluid cylinders at main reservoir pressure.

The operation of the draft gear is controlled by two valves, a directional valve and an air control valve. A locking device is located on each side of the draft gear, which locks the draft gear in either the retracted or extended position.

To move the draft gear, the directional valve should be placed in the desired position and the air control valve opened. The air will enter the top of the fluid supply cylinders, forcing the oil into the draft gear cylinder to move the draft gear "in" and "out."

The draft gear sidelock cylinders are spring loaded to hold the sidelocks in the locking position. Air is admitted to these cylinders when the air control valve is opened; the sidelocks will then move from the locking position and will stay in the unlocked position until the draft gear is in the desired position and the air control valve is closed.

Whistle valves are connected to the linkage of the locking cylinders and will whistle when the air control valve is opened. The whistle will continue to operate until the locking device is in the locked position.

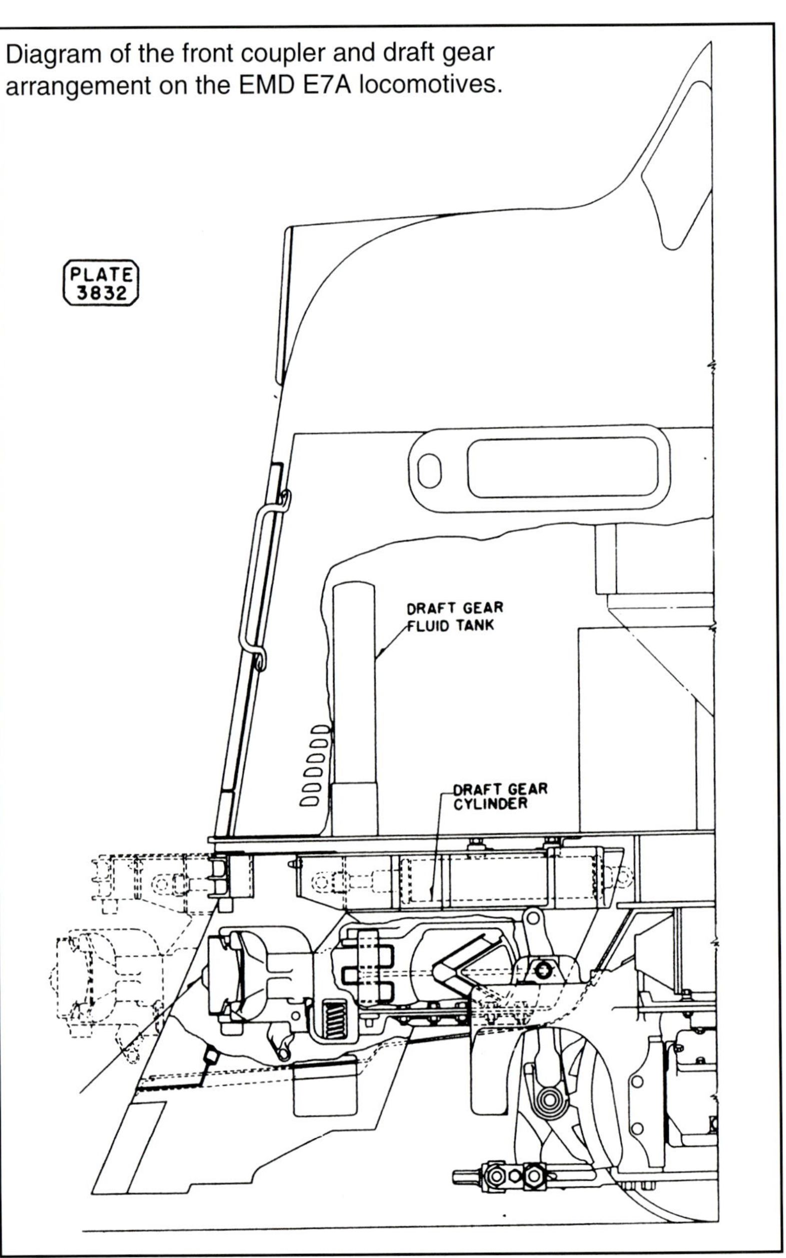

Diagram of the front coupler and draft gear arrangement on the EMD E7A locomotives.

E8 Photo Section

EMD, Hundman Publishing Coll.

B&O E8A No. 92 was donated to the B&O Museum in December 1993, and eventually will be repainted in its original paint scheme. It is shown here new at the EMD plant in 1950.

E8A — Model 2250 hp, Class DP-6

Road No.	Second Road No.	EMD Constr No.	Date Built	Disposition
90	1438	10231	9/50	EMD trade in 1972.
90A	1439	10232	9/50	Amtrak 200 1971, retired 1975, Naporano, scrap, 1975
92	(1440)	10233	9/50	Renumbered 1463 1969, became Amtrak 210, then DOT 210, 1975, went to Central Oklahoma Railfans, to B&O RR Museum in 1993.
92A	1441	10234	9/50	originally 1463, builders plates exchanged with 1440(1st) 1969, EMD trade in 1969
94	1442	12712	10/50	EMD trade in 1970.
94A	1443	12713	10/50	Amtrak 201 1971, retired 1975, Naporano Iron & Metal scrap 1976.
96	1444	12714	10/50	EMD trade in 1969.
96A	1445	12715	10/50	EMD trade in 1971.
26	1446	18675	10/53	Amtrak 202 1971, Naporano scrap 1975.
26A	1447	18676	10/53	Amtrak 203 1971, retired 1976, Chrome Crankshaft 1979.
28	1448	18677	10/53	Amtrak 204 1971, retired 1976, Naporano Iron & Metal scrap 1979.
28A	1449	18678	10/53	Amtrak 205 1971, retired 1976, Precision National 1979.
30	1450	18679	10/53	Amtrak 206 1971, retired 1976, Naporano Iron & Metal scrap 1975.
30A	1451	18680	11/53	Amtrak 207 1971, retired 1976, Naporano Iron & Metal scrap 1975.
32	1452	18681	11/53	Amtrak 208 1971, retired 1976, Naporano Iron & Metal scrap 1975.
32A	1453	18682	11/53	Amtrak 209 1971, retired 1976, Naporano Iron & Metalscrap 1975.

Westbound at 65 miles per hour, B&O E8A No. 1451 races across the diamond at Attica Junction, Ohio, on March 31, 1957.

With train at St. Louis is B&O E8A No. 1440, which became No. 1463 after a swap of builder's plates. June 20, 1958

E8 No. 1439 viewed broadside at Washington Union Station on June 27, 1971, shows no portholes, which often occurred as side sheets had to be replaced in carbody units.

(both) EMD, Hundman Publishing Coll.

Baltimore & Ohio
E8A No. 92

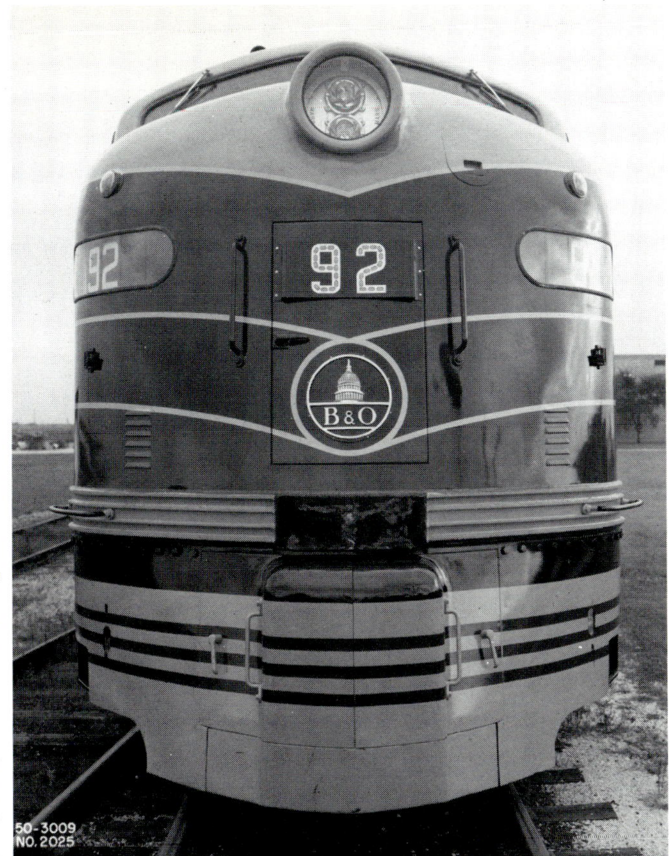

E8A No. 92, which is the subject of this book's cover, was built in September 1950, along with Nos. 90 and 90A. In 1957 it was renumbered to No. 1440 (1st) and was again renumbered in 1969 to No. 1463, and thus placed between two ex-C&O E8As, Nos. 4017 and 4007, B&O Nos. 1462 and 1464 respectively. In 1971 No. 92, then the 1463, went to Amtrak No. 210; four years later it became Department of Transportation No. 210, for use at its test facility at Pueblo, Colorado. Obtained by the Central Oklahoma Railfans, it kept the 210 number. It was obtained by the B&O Railroad Museum in Baltimore and went on display early in 1994.

An HO scale model of B&O E8A 92 is scheduled to be released by Life Like Models in 1994.

(Above) Builder's photo of front of Baltimore & Ohio E8A No. 92. Note the curved number boards, not like the E7 model. Also notice the Capitol Dome herald medalion bolted to the locomotive and the front number on a panel which was later removed. ***(Below)*** Left side 3/4 roster view taken by EMD at La Grange in September 1950. The most notable difference between the E7 and E8 aside from the grills and louvers behind the cab door is the roof area above the engines.

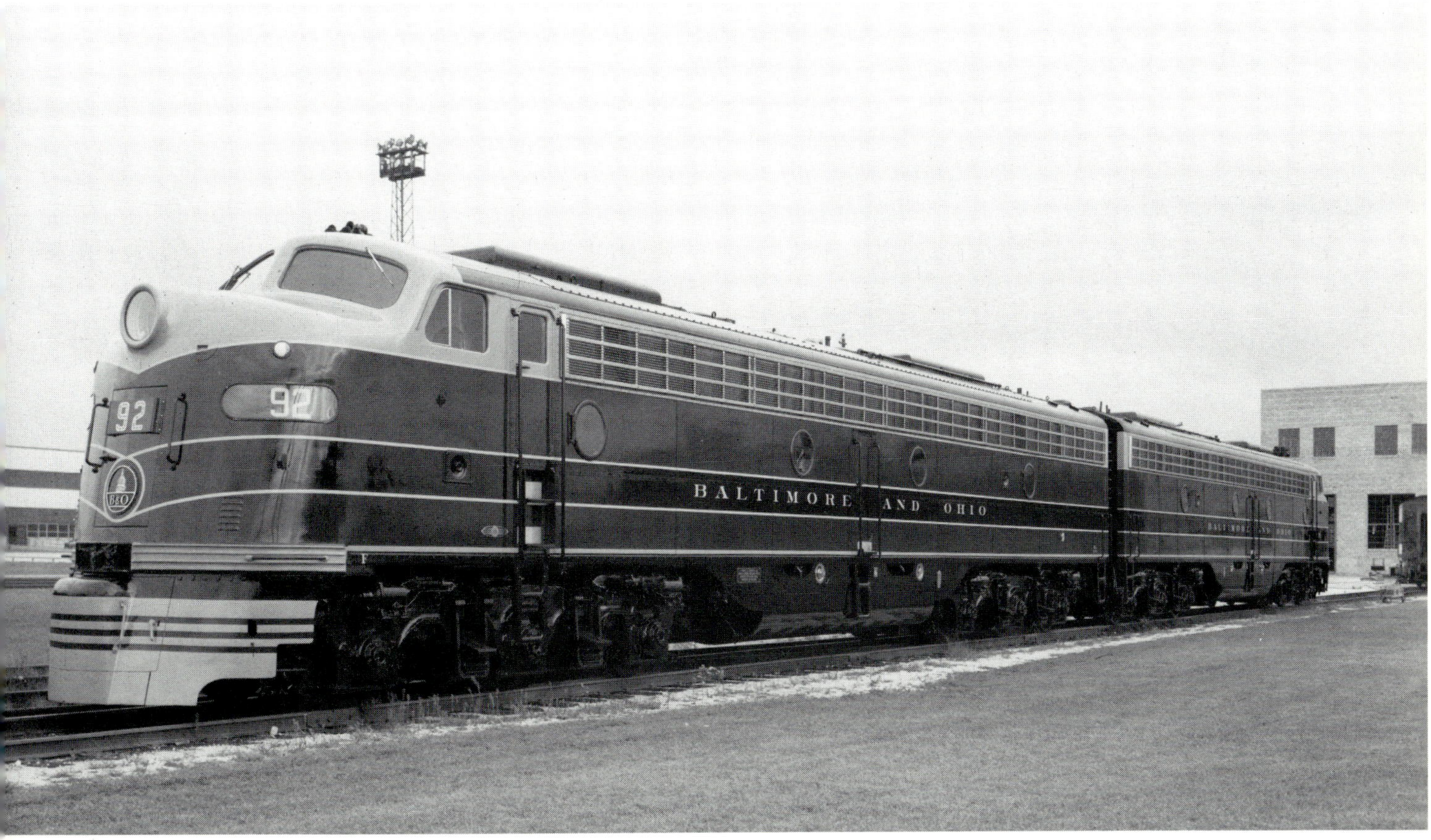

Louis A. Marre

The shortened *National Limited* in its later life on September 18, 1966, is powered by a single E8, No. 1450, at Winton Place, near Cincinnati.

On April 11, 1957, B&O E8A No. 1442 was on the head of a passenger train at Zanesville, Ohio. This locomotive is ideally lit for photography as one can see by all of the exterior details.

Paul Dunn, T. W. Dixon Coll.

E8 1451 in its all-blue dress, heads up the *Capitol Limited* at Chicago's Grand Central Station trainshed in August 1967, with the big "B&O" still adorning the station's Romanesque clock tower.

H. H. Harwood, Jr.

Former C&O E8 Photo Section

C&O Ry, C&O Hist. Soc. Coll.

(Above) A publicity photo at the time of the *Chesapeake & Ohio* and *Baltimore & Ohio* merger illustrates the slight differences in the front ends of an E7A, here a B&O unit, and an E8A, here the C&O unit. *(Left)* B&O E8A No. 1464 is ex-C&O No. 4007, seen here accelerating and kicking up dust from the gravel ballast, rolling east out of C&O's Fulton Yard in Richmond, Virginia, with Train No. 42, *The George Washington*, January 1970.

Doug Nuckles

E8A — Class DP-6, 2250 hp.

Road No.	Second Road No.	EMD Constr No.	Date Built	Disposition
C&O 4001	1460	14760	8/51	Transferred from C&O 1967, EMD trade-in 1972.
C&O 4011	1461	14770	11/51	Transferred from C&O 1967, EMD trade-in 1972.
C&O 4017	1462	14776	12/51	Transferred from C&O 1967, EMD trade-in 1972.
C&O-4006	1440(2nd)	14765	8/51	became 1st 1440 in 1957, to 1463, 1969, Amtrak 210, 1971, DOT 210, 1975, Central Oklahoma Railfans 210, B&O RR Museum 1993
C&O 4007	1464	14766	8/51	Transferred from C&O 1967, EMD trade-in 1972.
C&O 4009	1465	14768	8/51	Transferred from C&O 1967, EMD trade-in 1972.
C&O 4012	1466	14771	11/51	Transferred from C&O 1967, EMD trade-in 1972.
C&O 4013	1467	14772	11/51	Transferred from C&O 1967, Amtrak 211, 1971, sold Montour 1975.

R. Malinoski

(Above) B&O E8A No.1462, previously C&O No. 4017, is rolling along easy near Orleans Road, West Virginia, on November 1, 1968, with train No. 8, *The Shenandoah.*

(Left) Sometimes referred to as the "schizophrenic locomotive" because of the mistake in lettering, C&O E8A No. 4028, with five other E8s, was renumbered into the 1400 series with C&O lettering but a B&O herald on the nose. Seen here at Cumberland, Maryland, on March 11, 1972.

(both) Louis A. Marre Coll.

B&O E8A No. 1466, ex-C&O No. 4012, is at the Pittsburgh and Lake Erie station in Pittsburgh, on April 24, 1971. This down-on view shows some of roof details.

E8Am/E-8Bm Photo Section

Wearing the "sunburst" scheme, E8Am No. 1436 is ex-No. 55(2nd), built in August 1953 and rated at 2,000 horsepower. On March 29, 1964 it was leading train No. 2, *The Capitol Limited,* through Mitchell, Illinois. EMD classified the E8s that were built using a few components taken off traded-in EA's, so they were treated as rebuilds, in effect saying that they were upgraded EA's, but in fact they were full-fleged E8s, but rated at less horsepower because of the salvaged parts.

J. D. Ingles, L. A. Marre Coll.

Modernized B&O E8Am No. 1433 (built with parts from No. 51(2nd) is about to be turned on the table at Willard, Ohio, in April 1962.

H. H. Harwood, Jr.

E8Am — Model 2000 hp, Class DP-7

Road No.	Second Road No.	EMD Constr No.	Date Built	Disposition
51(2nd)	1433	(666)	12/53	All E8Am's were rated at 2,000 horsepower due to used parts from EA's. They were all traded in to EMD on SD40s in 1969-71.
53(2nd)	1434	(765)	10/53	
54(2nd)	1435	(766)	1/54	
55(2nd)	1436	(767)	8/53	
56(2nd)	1437	(800)	6/53	

The westbound *National Limited* is leaving Camden Station in Baltimore, in July 1965, behind E8Am No. 1435 and an E7A with modernized grills.

H. H. Harwood, Jr.

Posed in the classic 3/4 roster position, E8Am No. 1437, the last of five such units, is seen at Cincinnati, Ohio, on December 12, 1965.

Louis A. Marre

E8Bm — Model 2000 hp, Class DP-7X

Road No.	Second Road No.	EMD Constr No.	Date Built	Disposition
51X(2nd)	2414	(667)	10/53	EMD trade-in 1969, rated 2000 HP based on EA trade-in parts.
52X(2nd)	2415	(669)	5/53	EMD trade-in 1968, rated 2000 HP based on EA trade-in parts.
53X(2nd)	2416	(768)	5/53	EMD trade-in 1969, rated 2000 HP based on EA trade-in parts. sold to L&N, used to re-engine L&N ALCO switchers.
54X(2nd)	2417	(769)	8/53	EMD trade-in 1968, rated 2000 HP based onEA trade-in parts.
55X(2nd)	2418	(770)	11/53	EMD trade-in 1969, rated 2000 HP based on EA trade-in parts.
56X(2nd)	2419	(801)	1/54	EMD trade-in 1966, rated 2000 HP based on EA trade-in parts.

E9 Photo Section

(both) EMD, Hundman Publishing Coll.

Gary Stuebben

(Above) E9A No. 36 is shown just out of the EMD shop at La Grange, in a 3/4 roster view. The side view shows the model designation plate applied under the cab window. Above the B&O Capitol herald on the nose is the unit number applied on a metal plate.

(Above) E9 No. 1454 at Philiadelphia, fairly early in its career. It went on to Amtrak and was converted to a fuel tender before finally being sold for scrap in 1992.

(Left) It is May 1955 and this front view of E9A No. 36 at La Grange, shows off the clean curvaceous lines of the passenger locomotive model that made history all over the United States.

E9A — Class DP-8, 2400 hp,				
Road No.	Second Road No.	EMD Constr No.	Date Built	Disposition
34	1454	20377	5/55	became Amtrak 400, rebuilt as fuel tender, for sale 1992.
36	1455	20378	5/55	became Amtrak 401, retired 1981.
38	1456	20379	5/55	became Amtrak 402, scrapped, Precision National, 1981.
40	1457	20380	5/55	was to become Amtrak 403, retired 1975, scrapped 1976.

(Above) E9A No. 1456, with a matching E8Bm, has *The Capitol Limited* in tow, with several heavyweight head-end cars on May 21, 1964, at Walkerton, Indiana.

(Right) An E9A NO. 1454 and an E8A are on the ready track in Cleveland, Ohio, at West 3rd Street in March 1962. Both are in good paint, although the E8A has only one porthole on the left side.

B&O E9A No. 1454 only three years after the above photo waits on the ready track in Cincinnati, Ohio, on October 30, 1965 in the solid blue paint scheme. Ideal lighting conditions reveal that this unit is in good paint. The rear porthole on the left side has been replaced by new sheet metal.

Howard Ameling

In March 1965, E9 No. 1457 and a B unit with *The Capitol Limited* in Chicago. Four years later in 1969 when President Eisenhower's funeral train left Washington, D. C. for Kansas, it was pulled by No. 1457 and two E8s, C&O Nos. 4028 and 4016. All three locomotives were by then painted in the blue with lower gray panel paint scheme with large lettering on each side and yellow heralds on the nose. The train travelled to St. Louis over the B&O, where it was relieved by N&W geeps, then by UP E-units at Kansas City.

David Nyce, Gary Stuebben Coll.

E9A No. 1456 pauses with its train at Martinsburg, West Virginia, on July 12, 1958.

NOTE
The chart below indicates how many amperes of power a locomotive can "pull" during a period of time. This information was very important in determining how long an engine could run at a certain level of power output.

DIESEL ELECTRIC PASSENGER LOCOMOTIVES SHORT TIME RATINGS								
B&O Class and Numbers	Model	Continuous	60 Min. Zone	30 Min. Zone	15 Min. Zone	10 Min. Zone	5 Min. Zone	Make Back Trans.
PE2(1408-1414), PE2X(2407-2413)	E6	625	625-675	675-725	725-775	775-825	825-975	825
PE3(1415-1432,)	E7	625	625-675	675-725	725-775	775-825	825-975	825
PE5(1438-1453),PE5X(2414)	E8	750	750-825	825-875	875-950	950-1025	1025-1175	885
PE4(1433-1437),PE4X(2415-2419)	E8m	600	600-650	650-700	700-750	750-800	800-850	750
PE6(1454-1457)	E9	750	750-825	825-875	875-950	950-1025	1025-1175	1000

B&O, B&O Hist. Soc. Coll.

(Above) Train No. 27, *The Royal Blue*, on one of its last trips between New York and Washington, crosses the Squahanna River bridge on April 22, 1958 with E9 No. 1456 leading an E7 and eight cars.

(Below) Recently painted in the last C&O/B&O E-unit paint scheme, E9A No. 1456 is outside the Cumberland Shop on October 19, 1970.

R. Malinoski

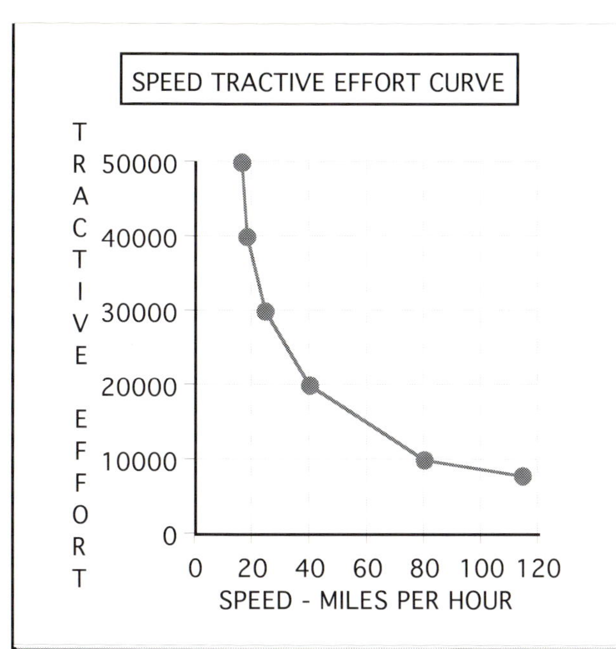

SPEED TRACTIVE EFFORT CURVE	
Tractive effort - pounds	Speed - miles per hour
50,000	16 mph
40,000	18 mph
30,000	25 mph
20,000	40 mph
10,000	80 mph
8,000	115 mph

The EMD E9 model locomotive offered a choice of four different gear ratios to meet a wide range of services. The E9 was able to meet conditions on a given railroad, but could be quickly and economically tailored to meet changing conditions at any time by simply changing gears and pinions.

E9 GEAR RATIO		
OPTION	GEARING	MAX. SPEED
1	57:20	85
2	56:21	92
3	55:22	98
4	52:25	117

Rolling along near Connellsville, Pennsylvania, on June 8, 1965, *The Diplomat* is westbound with E9A No. 1455, originally numbered 36, built in May 1955. R. Malinoski

H. H. Harwood, Jr.

Waiting to leave Camden Station in Baltimore, in August 1967, is B&O E9A No. 1455, with train No. 101, *The National Limited*. This was the last locomotive-hauled train scheduled for Camden Station.

B&O E9A No. 1456, in the all-blue paint scheme, leads *The Capitol Limited*, with the Strata-Dome car fifth, out of Grand Central Station, Chicago, about 1968.

R. C. Withers Coll.

Location of Parts — General Motors E8 and E9 Passenger Locomotives, A unit

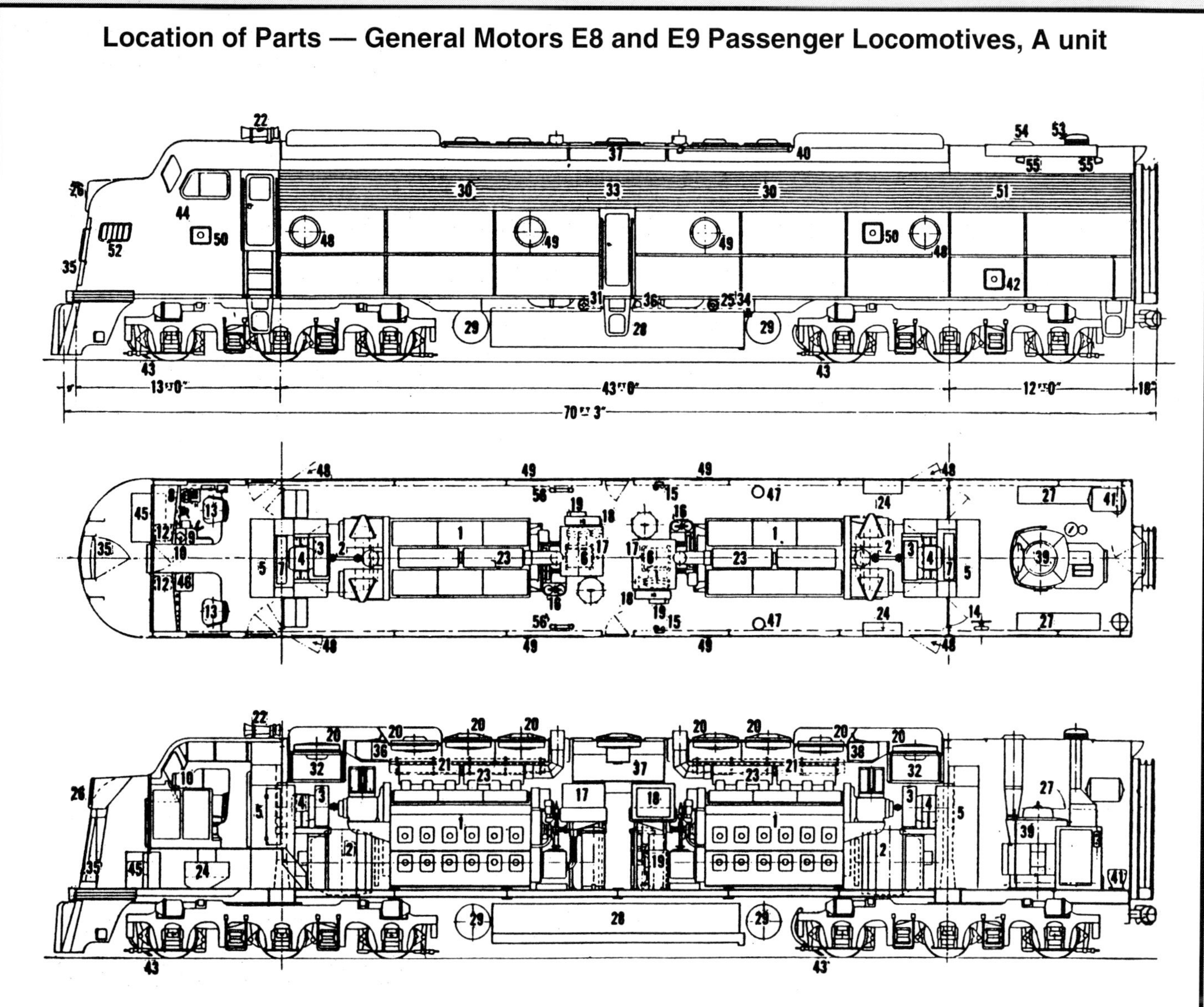

Drawing from *Locomotive Cyclopedia of American Practice*, 1950-1952, page 130.

Location of parts:
1. Engine—Model 12-567-B
2. Main generator & alternator
3. Generator blower
4. Aux. generator
5. Control cabinet
6. Air compressor
7. Traction motor blower
8. Instrument panel
9. Controller
10. Speedometer recorder
11. Air brake stand
12. Cab heater
13. Seat
14. Hand brake
15. Fuel tank vent with flame arrestor
16. Lub. oil filler
17. Engine water tank & lub. oil cooler
18. Engine control & instrument panel
19. Load regulator

20. Fan & Motor
21. Radiator
22. Horn
23. Exhaust manifold
24. Sand box
25. Fuel filter
26. Head light*
27. Batteries
28. Fuel (1,200gal water,1,200gal water)
29. Main air reservoir
30. Air intake & shutters
31. Boiler water filler
32. Engine room ventilator
33. Air intake for grids
34. Fuel tank gauge
35. Door (plain)
36. Emergency fuel cut-off
37. Dynamic break hatch*
38. A. C. contactor cabinet

39. Steam generator*
40. Air conpressor aftercooler
41. Toilet
42. Battery charging receptacle
43. Sanding nozzles
44. Blue flag bracket
45. Air brake rack
46. Water cooler*
47. M. P. pipe line filter
48. Hinged seat
49. Fixed sash
50. Sand box filler
51. Steam generator room shutters
52. Number box
53. Steam generator air intake
54. Steam generator stack
55. Battery box vents
56. Water tank vent

---

* Modifications

Amtrak

(both) T. W. Dixon

(Above) Amtrak train No. 643, *The Potomac Special,* is at Cumberland, on June 4, 1972, with E8A No. 200, ex-B&O No. 1439. When Amtrak was created it tried to select the best locomotioves for its initial use from the constituent railroads. B&O contributed 11 E8As and all four of its E9As. Most saw service until the mid 1970s when Amtrak had enough new power to release them, and they were almost all scrapped. Of the B&O units only one survived, Amtrak No. 210, which was previously B&O No. 1440 and before that No. 92. It has just been acquired by the B&O Railroad Museum for display as part of their collection.

(Right) B&O E8A No. 1455 (actually Amtrak No. 401) with the two car Amtrak train No. 642, *The Potomac Special*, arriving at Cumberland, Maryland, on May 21, 1972. In the days immedaitely following Amtrak's take-over of passenger service in the U. S., its trains looked pretty much as they did before the takeover, since the equipment contributed by the member railroads was used without repainting.

Modeling B&O E-Units in HO scale

Modelers desiring an E-unit in HO scale may be more fortunate now than ever before. Custom built brass models from the Orient have recently become available. While these are exquisitely detailed, they may need custom painting.

Life-Like Models will be importing an E8 model in several road names in spring of 1994. If this model is one of their better series, it may be detailed quite well. Walthers catalog lists E8A and B models in many road names. Models of E7As were available from Model Power several years ago. Heavy metal bodies of both E6s and E7s were available from Cary Locomotive Works and Bowser. Used models may occasionally be found for sale.

Challenger Imports, Ltd. will import a group of custom detailed and factory painted E7/8/9s, with only a few B units, to be ready in the spring of 1994. These are collectors' models including a limited number of B&O E8As in the classic blue and gray scheme.

For the do-it-yourself modelers there have been articles in the model railroad literature describing how to detail and custom paint HO models of E-units. Below is a list of detail parts that should be added to B&O models if not already present.

Modeler's Note:
Decals for painting and lettering B&O E-Units in HO scale are available from Microscale Industries, Inc., P. O. Box 11959, Costa Mesa, CA 92627. Appropriate paints are available from Floquil and Scalecoat companies.

E8A No. 30 on Army-Navy football game special train at Philadelphia in November 1955.   T. W. Dixon Coll.

Typical detail parts for E7,8,9

A Line (Proto Power West):
  29200 Windshield Wipers
Cal-Scale:
  316 Air horn
Detail Associates:
  1302 Cab sunshades
  1508 M.U. hoses
  1703 Clear 4' jewels
  2202 Grabirons
  220S Coupler lift bars
  2206 Lift ring eye bolts
  2505 Brass wire .015' dia.
Details West:
  118 Steam generator set
  157 Radio antenna
Walthers:
  429 Diaphragm
KaDee:
  7 Operating couplers
Microscale:
  87-396 Cab unlts
Scalecoat:
  1 Locomotive Black
  22 UP Yello (Imitation Gold)
  37 B&O Royal Blue
  41 Erie Lackawanna gray
  51 Flat Glaze
  54 Quick Dry
Testors:
  1160 Dullcote

References

1. Stover, J. F.: *History of the Baltimore & Ohio Railroad*, Purdue University Press, West Lafayette, IN, 1987.
2. Dilts, J. D.: The *Great Road, The Building of the B&O,The Nation's First Railroad*, Stanford University Press, 1993.
3. Drury, G. H.: *Historical Guide to North American Railroads*, Kalmbach Pub. Co., Milwaukee, WI, 1985.
4. Bruce, A. W.: *The Steam Locomotive in America*. W.W. Norton & Company, New York, 1952.
5. Kirkland, J. F.: *Dawn of the Diesel Age*, Interurban Press, Glendale, CA, 1983.
6. "Baltimore & Ohio Builds Steam Power for High Speed," *Railway Age*, May 4, 1935.
7. "Baltimore & Ohio Locomotive No. 5600," *Railway Age*, June 16, 1937.
8. Thompson, E. L.: "Highballing B&O Duplex-Drive," *Trains*, September 1964.
9. Hollingsworth, B.: *North American Locomotives*, Crown Publishers, Inc., London, 1984.
10. Shaffer, F. E.: "Helper Turn out of M&K Junction," *Trains*, Sept., 1960.
11. Reck, F. M.: *The Dilworth Story,* McGraw-Hill Book Co., New York, 1954.
12. Reck, F. M.: *On Time,* Electro-Motive Division of General Motors Corporation, La Grange, IL, 1948.
13. Hundman, R. L.: "EMD E-6 Early Production Passenger Unit," *Mainline Modeler,* March 1983.
14. Urbach, H. H.: "Diesel-Locomotive Operation," *Railway Age*, July 15, 1939.
15. Gurley, F. G.: "New Technologies in Transport," *Railway Age*, 1940.
16. "Long Diesel Locomotive Run," *Railway Age*, page 378, September 21, 1935.
17. "B&O 3,600 HP Diesel-Electric, No. 51," *Railway Age*, page 1004-5, June 16, 1937.
18. "Fourth B&O Diesel on Delivery List," *Railway Age*, page 210, January 22, 1938.
19. "B&O Places Diesels on N.Y.-Capital Runs," *Railway Age*, page 86, July 9, 1938.
20. 'Modernized *Capitol Limited* Placed in Service," *Railway Age*, page 790, November 26, 1938.
21. "B&O Diesel on the Job 365 Days in a Year," *Railway Age*, page 469, March 9, 1940.
22. "B&O Now Has Five Diesel-Driven Trains, *Railway Age*, page 449, September 28, 1940.
23. "B&O Operates Diesel Fleet, *Railway Age*, page 738, November 16, 1940.
24. 'B&O Inaugurates Diesel Service to Detroit, *Railway Age*, page 214, August 2, 1941.
25. Kamm, A. L. Jr and Morgan D. P.: "Those Esthetic E's," *Trains* , pages 22-27, May 1964.
26. Sagle, L. W., Staufer, A. F.: *B&O Power*, Staufer Publishing Co., Inc,
27. Reed, R. C.: *The Streamline Era*, Golden West Books, San Marino, CA, 1975.
28. Harwood, H. H. Jr.: *Royal Blue Line*, Greenberg Publishing Co., Inc., Sykesville, MD, 1987.
29. "Modernized Trains Ring the Bell," *Railway Age*, November 16, 1940.
30. Hartley, S.: "An Exposition of E's, Part I," *Passenger Train Journal*, June/July 1986.
31. Hartley, S.: "An Exposition of E's, Part II," *Passenger Train Journal*, August 1986.
32. *Instruction Manual for Operation of Railway Equipment, B&O Nos. 52, 57-59*, EMD, La Grange, IL, July 1941.
33. *Instruction Manual for Operation of Railway Equipment, B&O Nos. 60-63*, EMD, La Grange, IL, September1941.
34. *Passenger Locomotive Operating Manual No. 2300, B&O E7's*, EMD, La Grange, IL, April 1945.
35. *Diesel Locomotive Operating Manual No. 2311, Model E8*, EMD, General Motors, La Grange, IL, 1951.
36. *Locomotive Cyclopedia of American Practice*, Simmons-Boardman Publishing Corp, New York, 1952.
37. Meyer, Bruce: "B&O E-Unit Painting Guide," *Mainline Modeler*, March 1983.
38. Hayden, R.: *Diesel Locomotive Cyclopedia No. 2*, Kalmbach Publishing Co., Milwaukee, 1980.
39. *General Motors Diesel Locomotive Catalog*, 1950.
40. *General Motors Diesel Locomotive Catalog*, 1953-1954.
41. *Diesel-Electric Locomotive Short Time Ratings*, Baltimore & Ohio Railroad Company, October 1, 1955.
42. *Renumbering and Reclassification of Locomotives and Diesel Rail Motor Cars*, B&O RR Co., November 1, 1956.
43. *Diesel-Electric Locomotives: Questions and Answers on Machinery and Operations*, B&O RR Co., June 1959.
44. Cuisinier, W. A.: "The E7, E8, E9 compared," *Extra 2200 South*, November/December, 1973.
45. Eck, H. E., and McElvany, A. W.: "Diesel Operation on the B&O," personal communication, November 3, 1993.
46. Holt, J. J.: "Diesel Electric Supervisors," in personal letter, November 15, 1993.
47. Harwood, H. H., Jr.: "B&O History and Passenger Train Operations," personal letter, December 11, 1993.
48. Howes, W. F., Jr.: "B&O Locomotives and Passenger Trains," personal communication, December 14, 1993.